ROPLEY—Past and Present

This story of the village of Ropley typifies the way an English village grows and changes through the manifold activities of its inhabitants—how its life and vigour are simply a reflection of the dynamism of those who dwell in it. A Hampshire story—commissioned by The Ropley Society—which is far more than just another local interest book.

THE ROPLEY SOCIETY

The Ropley Society was founded in 1985 as unofficial watchdog to 'protect and enhance' the amenities of the village of Ropley in co-operation with the local authorities. The Chairman, Sir Frederick Mason KCVO CMG, came to the village in 1975 after a long and distinguished career in the diplomatic service. In 1980 he founded the East Hampshire Branch of the Council for the Protection of Rural England (CPRE). His narrative is based on documents prepared over the years by local residents—now edited and brought up-to-date.

ROPLEY

PAST AND PRESENT

A Brief Story of a Hampshire Village

compiled and edited by
FREDERICK MASON

Line Drawings by Alan Thomas

First edition published in 1989 by Scriptmate Editions, 11 Rosemont Road, London NW3 6NG for the Ropley Society

Distributed by the Ropley Society, The Forge, Ropley, Hampshire SO24 0DS

ISBN: 0 9514647 0 1 (hbk); 0 9514647 1 X (pbk)

Line drawings ©Alan Thomas 1989
Colour photograph of Ropley village, F Sherwin Green

Designed by Scriptmate Editions and composed on Rank Xerox XPS701 electronic publishing system by Scan Laser Ltd
The book laser printed by Scan Laser Ltd, 16/22 Epworth Street, London EC2A 4DL on Rank Xerox 9790 and 4090 laser printers
Additional litho offset printing by Lavengro Print Ltd, London

As Shade doth pass from Line to Line
By Motion of the Sun;
So doth our Age from Time to Time
Until our Race is Run

inscription on the 17th century sundial
at Ropley House

PREFACE

This book owes its existence largely to the memories and narratives of three residents of Ropley who were devoted to the village and gave much of their time to studying its history and customs. They were—in order of appearance—Miss Marianne Hagen who published the well-known *Annals of Old Ropley* in 1929 and died soon after; Mr A.E. Guy who served the village for many years in official and unofficial capacities until his death in 1967; and Mr J.A.L. Webb who knew and travelled this countryside, and had a deep sense of history, and died in 1974. The two latter compiled extensive notes which have fortunately been preserved and are hereby gratefully acknowledged.

But the story of a village like Ropley is a moving one in more senses than one, and I have also called upon many others to bring the story up-to-date. In doing so I have been constantly urged to widen and deepen these enquiries by calling upon more and more people and sources. Sadly life is too short, and it seemed to me preferable to 'publish and be damned', rather than face long delays. Perhaps someone else will pick up the threads...

Inevitably, therefore, there are gaps and, perhaps, some inaccuracies, though I have tried to keep the latter to a minimum.

I trust that those (and there are quite a few) who have helped with advice and information will forgive me if I do not name them individually. I have, however, made use of a published text, which I acknowledge with thanks. It is Mr R.J.R. Sawyer's excellent leaflet, *The History of St Peter's Church* (to be found in the church).

A special word of thanks is due to Mrs Webb who so kindly lent me her late husband's manuscript (covering also the Parish of Four Marks and West Tisted), and to Dr John Happel who preserved and made available the notes compiled by Albert Guy.

Finally my warm thanks are also due to the East Hampshire District Council, Ropley Parish Council, and the Willie and Mabel Morris Charitable Trust which, through their generous help and encouragement, have made possible the publication of this book through the Ropley Society.

Frederick Mason
Chairman, Ropley Society
June 1989

CONTENTS

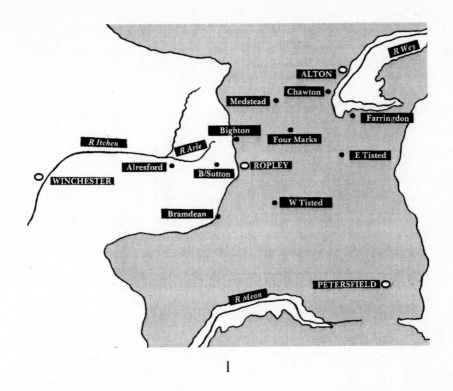

I

A BRIEF INTRODUCTION TO THE COUNTRYSIDE

The Parish of Ropley in East Hampshire lies between the main A31 (the old Turnpike Road) from Winchester to Alton and the minor C18 road branching off the A31 to Petersfield via Hedge Corner on the A 32. The village, which covers an area of about twelve square miles, is situated on the western slopes of a ridge running approximately south to north and forming a watershed separating the basins of the Wey and the Meon rivers from those of the Arle and Itchen.

Originally the ecclesiastical and political boundaries included Four Marks in the Parish of Ropley. A 'mark' was a stake stone or tree, indicating a boundary, and in this case marked the joining of the parishes of Medstead, Chawton, Farringdon and Ropley. Ropley parish was bounded to the north by Bighton and Medstead, to the east by

11

Chawton, Farringdon and East Tisted, to the south by West Tisted and to the west by Bramdean and Bishop's Sutton. The eastern and western halves of the parish were separated by the ridge, and from earliest times the two parts developed their separate identities, although united on the political map.

The division can broadly be seen in the agricultural and geological composition of the land. The western half of the original parish is composed of good farm and pasture land with a deep chalk layer covered with a skin of good brown soil. The higher land to the east and south is well wooded where the chalkdowns slope down towards Farringdon and Selborne. Originally this was part of the great Andredsweald forest which extended from the ridge into Sussex and part of Surrey. Alice Holt and Woolmer (Wolves Marsh) are the only extensive woods that remain in Hampshire of this once great forest. At Ropley we still have the much depleted Old Down Wood, Dogford Wood, Charlwood, Winchester Wood and Stoney Brow, this last with its beautiful avenue leading down to Hedge Corner.

In the west the farmlands have been described by William Cobbett (1822) in his *Rural Rides* as being of a 'deep loam bordering on clay, rich in colour and full of yellow looking stones. On this rich and heavy land the wheat was good.' Despite the continual turning over of the land, these large yellow stones still persist in coming to light. Cobbett also remarked on some fine swedes he saw on Ropley Dean.

This soil is also suitable for horticulture and the village has been noted for its fine flowers. As a result, bee-keeping once flourished here. The honey was used in olden times for the production of mead and it is said that William the Conqueror obtained his honey in Ropley. Unfortunately this industry has declined in recent years.

Surface water has almost disappeared in the district, though dew-ponds can still be seen at Charlwood and Monkwood. In Ropley the only remaining pond at the top of Church Street is believed to be declining in spite of local efforts to restore and improve it. There were other ponds at The Dean and at Chase Farm in Gilbert Street and at Andrews Lane, fed from rain waters descending from Swelling Hill. But the ponds have been filled in and a moderate shower of rain can now cause flooding in Gascoigne Lane. The last pond to be filled in was at Church Farm in Church Street. Just outside the parish boundary is the largest pond in the area, at Kitwood, the highest point between Ropley and Four Marks, and just beyond the apex of Swelling Hill.

It is a peculiarity of chalk downland that there are few surface streams, and yet there are ample sources for strongly flowing rivers like the Wey, Meon and Itchen. This is due to the geological construction of the downs. Under a skin of loam, there is a stratum of coarse chalk impregnated with the yellow stones mentioned by William Cobbett Below this stratum lies another layer of chalk, this time of a finer texture free of stones. This layer rests on a bed of clay impervious to water. Rain falling on the downs percolates through the chalk strata down to the clay bed. It then builds upwards saturating the lower levels of chalk. The water now seeks its lowest level flowing over the clay strata until the chalk narrows and the saturation level reaches the surface and the water appears in the form of springs. At Ropley these springs were originally exposed on the Dean. In the 1930s and 40s they could be seen rising on the grass verges opposite the Anchor Inn.

MARLING AND THE DELLS

Stretching across the ridge in a line from West Tisted and Privett to Medstead is a line of dells, some large and others just a depression in the ground. Some of the larger ones are bordered by trees. These were apparently dug for the purpose of marling (lime fertilising) the nearby land. In olden days when marling was done by hand a dell would be opened to cater for adjacent land. When the distance became too great for returning to it on foot another dell was opened. In later (feudal) times, the land was cultivated in strips (lynches) and the yeoman would dig a dell for his own strip and these dells became very numerous. Then in course of time chalk quarries were cut for marling from wagons and chalk quarrying for agriculture became a widespread industry. Ropley's local quarry is in Soames Lane.

II

THE ORIGINS AND GROWTH OF ROPLEY

The earliest evidence of human existence in the Ropley area is from the later Bronze Age (about 1000 BC). Two examples are as follows:

The Barrow

A solitary late Bronze Age Barrow stood in an open field to the west of Old Down Wood. It has now been levelled by the plough, but some residents of today remember viewing it from Brislands Lane. It was the type known as a Bowl Barrow from its resemblance to an inverted bowl. The barrows of Hampshire have not been explored (as were those in Wiltshire) and there is no record of this one having been opened. The Bowl Barrow is the simplest form of Round Barrows, the majority of which were used to inter the remains of some distinguished person. The earlier ones revealed the corpses to be lying in a foetal position, but the later ones contained cremated remains together with pottery and arms.

Ropley people used to say that a battle was fought here, but there is no evidence of this. The deceased in the Bowl Barrow may have been killed while hunting. His people might have interred him with due ceremony on the spot. Other similar barrows have been found at Medstead, Bighton and Kilmeston.

The Torque

In 1845 a beautiful gold torque was ploughed up at Lyewood. The discovery does not, in itself, verify the existence of a Bronze Age settlement or burial ground, as has been suggested. The usual torque is normally a length of square section metal rod twisted along its length and curved in a rough circle of about ten inches diameter, with its ends re-curved so that it fits around the neck. The Lyewood specimen is similar, but it is rolled again in a spiral apparently adapted for the wrist. This beautiful ornament weighed over five ounces and was exhibited by Mr Lilywhite on whose ground it was found, at a meeting of the Archeological Institute in Winchester in 1845.

For a number of years it was preserved at Lyewood, after which it passed into the collection of Sir John Evans, whose son Sir Arthur Evans sold it at Sothebys in 1925 to the Cornwall County Museum at Truro. It dates from the Late Bronze Age, about 1000-800 BC, and is a type common in Britain but exceptional abroad.

A replica of the original torque has been made and this is now in the Curtis Museum in Alton.

BEGINNINGS OF THE VILLAGE

There is no evidence of a settled community at the time of the Belgae (about 50 BC) but it is very probable that some families may have settled in the Dean. Roman ruins have been found near Bighton and Bramdean, but only coins have been found in Ropley. A Roman road may have existed here.

There is much evidence, however, that the Saxons lived in or around the present area of Ropley and a stone coffin of the Saxon period was unearthed near the Soke during the excavation of the railway and is preserved in St Peter's Church.

SAXON PLACE NAMES

The name of the village of Ropley is considered to be Anglo-Saxon, but there is difference of opinion as to the original meaning. The Rev J.B. Johnston in his book *The Place Names of England and Wales* describes the name as Old English *lea,* a meadow, measured by a rope. Other sources refer to the Anglo-Saxon *ley* or *legh,* originally meaning a wood and later an open glade in a wood. Nowadays in some farming circles the word means a wide open space for grazing.

This particular *ley* is believed to take its name from the thane or chieftain who held the land at that time, whose name was probably Hroppa. In support of this theory, the Bishop of Winchester, Dr A.T.P. Williams, speaking at a meeting of the Hampshire Local History Council at Eastleigh in December 1956, said, 'People had often given their names to places, particularly those who had owned the places.' The Bishop also explained the meaning of the word *leigh* to be a clearing in a wood—'the sort of place where there were trees and also room for fairly level grazing'.

The name of the village has never been consistently spelt. It has appeared as Ropelia in the 12th century, Roppele and Roppeleghe in the 14th century and Ropeley in the 15th. Even with maps the cartographers fail to agree. Early maps were authorised by Queen Elizabeth in 1579 when Christopher Saxton attempted to map the whole country. On a map of Hampshire signed by Saxton and dated 1575 the village is shown as Ripley in the Sutton Hundred. Considering the primitive methods used in those days, the position of Ropley and its neighbours on this map are extremely accurate. A map by John Speed in 1610 spells the name as Ropley, as does Morden in 1695, while T. Kitchen in 1738 reverts to Ripley.

In the present Post Office Directory this is the only village in the country to bear the name of Ropley.

ROPLEY DEAN

Den or *dean* in Anglo-Saxon means an open glade bordering woodland. The borders of Andredsweald forest may be traced by such names as Bramdean, Bordean, Brockwood Dean and Ramsdean.

THE STREETS

The word 'street' is more likely to have derived from the Saxon *straet* than the Latin *strata*. *Straet* refers to a road or way including the houses and buildings bordering it, or a hamlet. Ropley was originally made up of such hamlets, for example North Street, South Street, Church Street and Gilbert Street.

ROPLEY SOKE (Anglo-Saxon *soc* or *soca* — Liberty).

Nestling comfortably in an open bowl formation sculpted out of the steep, western flank of the Four Marks escarpment lies the half-timbered Watercress Inn, formerly known as The Shant Inn; nearby are two buildings and another restored cottage—all that remain of the former hamlet of Ropley Soke. In former times (before the extension of the main road from Four Marks), access to this hamlet would have been by foot over the downs from Brislands Cottages in Brislands Lane. These cottages have now shared the fate of those in the Soke and have crumbled to dust.

In medieval times the civic affairs of the village were administered by the Courts Leet at Alresford or the County Court at Winchester. Parallel to the administration of the civic courts was a government of the Bishops over their own territories, the Liberties or Sokes. The tything or borsman, the headman of a hamlet, was the representative at the Ecclesiastical or Bishop's Court held in Cheyney Court at Winchester Cathedral under the Bailiff of the Soke. Government was directly by the Bishop and civic authorities had no power in the Soke. Other examples are Winchester Soke (Chesil or Cheesehill) and Alresford Soke (at the bottom of Broad Street, comprising the neighbourhood of the Weirs). This form of government was abolished in the 19th century.

DOMESDAY BOOK

Ropley is not mentioned in Domesday Book but it formed part of the administrative *Hundred of Bishop's Sutton*. Besides the vill of Ropley this included the parishes of Bighton, Bramdean, West Tisted and, for some obscure reason, Headley near Bordon. Headley was transferred to the Alton Hundred in the 19th century.

At the time of the Domesday survey the Bishop's Sutton Hundred was entered as the *Hundred of Esselei*. It was then larger in area, extending from Swarraton in the north to West Tisted and Bramdean, and west as far as Tichbourne and part of Alresford. It is not known when the name of Esselei disappeared and the title of Bishop's Sutton substituted, but the Hundred was reduced to the six vills at the same time. Bishop's Sutton was known variously as Sudtone (11th century); Suttone Bishop (13th century); Sutton Bishops and Sutton Episcopi in the 14th century. The parish included the headwaters of the River Arle and Ropley was included as a vill with its own chapel. In 1551 the Lord of Bishop's Sutton was said to be the chief Lord of Ropley, and in subsequent years he was known as the Lord of Sutton-cum-Ropley or of Sutton-Ropley.

The Hundred had passed into the ownership of the Bishops of Winchester in the 12th century and William of Wykeham, Bishop of

17

Winchester, as Lord of the Hundred, had built a palace at Bishop's Sutton and founded the 'Saynte Marie College of Wynchestre'. In 1402 he made over large parts of Sutton and Ropley to the College, to whom they still belong today. The Bishops of Winchester remained Lords of the Hundred until 1869 when the title was taken over by the Ecclesiastical Commissioners. Shortly afterwards the Chapel of Ropley, which had been annexed to the parish church of Bishop's Sutton at an early date, became a separate parish by Order in Council in August 1882.

By about the middle of the 19th century Ropley parish covered a large area, some 4,600 acres in 1851 with a population of 818. The parish then consisted of several hamlets scattered round the central part of the village surrounding the church; these included Kelwood (now Kitwood), Chalwood (now Charlwood), Ropley Dene, Gilbert Street and Lyeway. In 1932 about 900 acres of land on the eastern side of the parish became part of the newly formed Civil Parish of Four Marks.

In 1851 transport around the village and to places outside the parish would, of course, have been entirely on foot or horseback or by horse drawn vehicles, so most of the inhabitants would not have travelled far from the village. The main road (now the A31) was on the route taken by some of the London-Southampton and Guildford-Southampton coaches. This road originally ran slightly farther south than it does at present, following one of the main routes of the Pilgrims' Way from Winchester to Guildford, with two inns, the Chequers and the Anchor, providing refreshment for travellers.

The village, though not as isolated as many, must have been largely self-supporting, especially before the Alton-Winchester railway arrived in the 1860s. The Directories give two lists of the principal residents of the village, one of 'Private Residents' and one of Traders, later called the Commercial List. In 1851 there were five private residents and some twenty tradesmen. These included seven farmers and various trades allied to farming, such as wheelwrights, a butcher and a corn dealer. Other trades listed were publicans, carpenters, a plumber and glazier, a baker, two shopkeepers (with bakeries), a tailor and a shoemaker. By 1867 several other tradesmen were listed including a churn maker, a basket and sieve maker and a draper, and by 1878 a land measurer, timber dealer, maltster and bricklayer were included in the list, also a thrashing machine owner, who later was listed as a timber merchant and sawmill proprietor.

The development of the village in the latter half of the 19th century owed much to the building of the railway and the existence of the Hampshire Hunt, and by 1911 the list of 'Private Residents' had grown to 30 (of whom six were listed as living in Four Marks). Amongst the 60 on the Commercial List was a doctor, and new trades included a coal merchant, cycle repairers, a motor engineer—also several poultry farmers, and a Ropley and District Poultry and Egg Society had been formed. By the end of the 1914-18 war the population was nearly 1,500, many of these being in the Four Marks end of the parish, and many living in scattered small houses and bungalows which were being built, especially in the Monkwood and Soames and Stapley Lane area and at Four Marks. After the formation of a separate parish at Four Marks in 1932, the area of Ropley was reduced to 3,704 acres, with a population of 1,090.

By 1939 the character of the village had changed very much from the village of 1851. Agriculture and allied farming trades were still the principal occupations of the inhabitants, but with improving transport and communications there was much more contact with other towns and villages. Many people with no previous local connections had come to live in the village, either those working in Alton and Alresford, or those who retired to the country. Unfortunately, there was very little control of local planning, and this led to the random building of houses and bungalows over a large area, many of a temporary nature.

Ropley is now one of the largest villages in Hampshire, with a population of well over 1500 (1135 on the 1988 electoral roll) and two main centres, one around the parish church and north Conservation Area, and the other at Ropley Dean on the A31. A south Conservation Area has also been designated around South Street and on the Petersfield Road (the C18) and much housing development has taken place largely in the form of ribbon development along most of the roads in the parish, particularly at Monkwood, Parkstone Road, Stapley Lane and Soames Lane, Petersfield Road and Gascoigne Lane.

The village is nowadays well served on the whole with main bus services along the A31 and occasional and voluntary services to Petersfield, Alton and Alresford. There is a flourishing primary school in Church Street, a doctors' surgery near Ropley Dean covering a wide area, two general stores at Pondside near the church and at Ropley Dean (the latter also a Post Office), one filling station, two repair garages, and four public houses. The centre near St Peter's Church includes the coffee room, Parish Hall and Recreation Ground and a number of attractive old houses, a well-designed council estate and other homes of recent construction. The Mid-Hants Steam Railway (The Watercress Line) has its small station and main locomotive sheds north of the A31, but otherwise there is little in the way of light industry, the village having retained its mainly agricultural character.

St Peter's Church, Ropley

III

THE PARISH CHURCH OF ST PETER

Throughout the centuries the English parish church or chapel has been the communal centre around which the life of the people revolved, and in this respect St Peter's Church at Ropley is no exception.

At the time of the Domesday Survey of 1085 the administrative Hundred of Esselei consisted of 'Sudtone' (Sutton), the great landowner Count Eustace's domain of 25 hides and a church (the original of St Peter's), held from King William I. It also included seven hides and a church at West Tisted. In 1115 the Augustan Priory of Merton in Surrey was founded and Count Eustace endowed it with the church and great tithes from his holding. About 1150 a daughter church was built on the western edge of the parish (at what had become known as Bishop's Sutton) and dedicated to the popular saint of that time, St Nicholas. Thereafter the development of the two churches at Ropley and Bishop's Sutton ran parallel for 800 years until the original parish was divided into Ropley and Bishop's Sutton in 1882. After a further century the two parishes, together with West Tisted, have again become a united benefice.

The original 11th century early Norman church where St Peter's now stands appears to have been cruciform in shape, and the only remaining visible Norman feature is the door to the present south transept, although part of the south and west walls appear to be original. Extensions to the church were made with the expansion of local trade and farming in the 13th century and a narrow south chapel was added, as well as the arcade to the south transept The church at this time was served by the Canons of Merton Priory.

The bell tower was built at the end of the 14th century at the time when William of Wykeham was endowing Winchester College with part of the manor of Ropley. It marked a change in emphasis in worship, as the bells for the first time cheerfully summoned the ordinary people of the parish to the services. The tower is typical of Hampshire churches in the use of wood for structural purposes. The south wall of the 13th century chapel and the east wall and roof of the Norman south transept had to be pulled down to allow two of the massive timber uprights of the tower to be erected within the transept. The strong square tower was then completed by the erection of the two easterly uprights and enclosed by widening the chapel whose east wall was extended southwards plus a new window. A new south wall was built on the present lines, and the ogee-headed south window and the piscina also date from this period.

Greater involvement in worship by the people is also reflected in the 15th century by attention being turned to the nave when the west window was enlarged and a new south door installed. The stoup on this door marks the introduction of mysticism to the people and the closer ties of priest and people are shown by the provision of a font. Further improvements to the nave were made in the early 16th century by which time the church would have been graced by a rood screen. The church seems to have attained its maximum splendour of decoration and colour by the end of the 15th century.

With the 16th century came the Reformation, and the church registers date from the time when Thomas Cromwell ordered them to be kept in 1538. This was a period of turmoil, during which the stone altar was replaced by a portable table and the rood screen and south chapel dismantled. All crucifixes and candles were forbidden and the Bible and Prayer Book printed in English were used.

Three hundred years after the first ring of bells was installed, the bell frame was renewed in 1701 and 'John Gilberd did contrive to cast from four this peel of five'. Extensive improvements took place about this time, including a new roof and a singing gallery against the west wall. In the centre of the church stood a panelled pulpit and the whole floor area was filled with box pews. The Royal Arms which display the lilies of France in their first quarter, are of this period (before 1707) although overpainted 'G.III 1791'. Such arms were first ordered to be set up in the churches in 1534, during the reign of Henry VIII.

Towards the end of the 18th century the gallery was further extended and the pulpit moved into the centre of the church and raised on posts enabling William Howley, the vicar, to see into and be seen from every corner of the church.

Further extension of the seating capacity became necessary in Victorian times half a century later when an extension on the north side of the church was built and filled with more box pews. The pulpit was again moved and placed against the east wall on the south side of the altar.

Dramatic changes took place at the end of the 19th century when an inspection of the building caused concern. The Rev W.H. Leak had been appointed vicar in 1891, having been faced with a similar problem at Bishop's Sutton. A restoration committee was formed in 1894 and funds raised through an appeal from the vicar. The gallery, box pews, old pulpit and rails were torn out and destroyed. The plaster ceilings were pulled down, the roofs stripped off, the north wall of the nave was demolished and the floors ripped up.

To plans prepared by Charles Miles FRBA the north aisle and arcade were extended westwards, the west gable refaced and raised to its original height and a chancel arch and east gable to the nave were built. The roofs were renewed, the four stout posts to the tower underpinned with concrete, buttresses built, windows replaced, walls refaced and the porch rebuilt. A thorough rebuilding in the Victorian manner.

On completion the church was furnished with chairs and a new pulpit, choir stalls in the chancel and new altar rails, and a service of dedication took place on 27th April 1897 when the sermon was preached by the Bishop of Guildford and the choir appeared for the first time in cassocks and surplices.

In 1911 a new organ built by Mr Binns of Leeds was installed in the north aisle and the old 14th century chapel was used as a vestry.

The fine church as we see it today has thus gone through centuries of change culminating in a massive 'renovation' at the end of the last century, which sadly destroyed much of its ancient charm. In spite of two devastating world wars it has been maintained with loving care by generations of vicars and parishioners. During the 60s and 70s special fund raising was successful in dealing with such problems as death watch beetle in the roof timbers, installing such amenities as central heating and carrying out general restoration in 1971. In 1981 the Friends of St Peter's Association was formed on the initiative of Dr John Happel and has since been remarkably successful in accumulating funds for future major maintenance, and for on-going improvements to the church, the churchyard and the adjacent Coffee Room. An Organ Fund has also been established under the auspices of the Parochial Church Council for a major overhaul expected by the end of the century.

Features of today's church include the following:

THE REREDOS made in English Oak has six panels and a canopy with three shields inscribed 'IHS' and carved with bunches of grapes. Messrs Laverty of Winchester executed the work on subscriptions raised by Mrs Wynne of Ropley Lodge and dedicated to the memory of her daughter Joan (who died in 1919) on 7th February 1942, by Bishop Taylor Smith, Chaplain General to the Forces.

THE CHURCH BELLS: At the time of the restoration in 1896 it had always been thought that the bells had been cast in a field outside the church, but the discovery of the foundry under the floor of the south transept revealed that the casting had actually taken place there.

The original inscriptions of the five bells were:
I as treble doo beggin S.K. 1701
Fear God, Honnare the King S.K. 1701
Samuel Knight mead this ring
Robert Gatlin of London Fecit 1749
Unto this church I doo you call
Death to the grave will somans all
John Gilberd did contrive to cast from four this
        peal of FIFE (Five)

In 1927 the third bell was found to be cracked and all the bells were recast by Messrs Gillett and Johnston of Croydon, and the original inscriptions copied. A new treble bell was added making a peal of six. This bell was inscribed, 'To the Glory of God and in memory of Jacob and Mary Hagen, also P.G.W., J.S.O'H., and A.H.S. The gift of M. S. Hagen, 1927'.

A brass tablet on the south wall of the nave under the bell tower is inscribed: 'To commemorate the gift of Marianne Sophia Hagen for the restoration of the church bells and the provision of a new treble bell.

24

This brass is dedicated by grateful parishioners, 1927':

THE WAR MEMORIALS: The names of the numerous men of Ropley who fell in the two World Wars are inscribed on two handsome tablets of Carrara marble flanking the chancel arch, as follows:

World War 1914-1918

Pte Walter Barnes	11th Hants
Pte Norman R. Bluett	1st Hants
Lce Cpl. Walter Bone	2nd 4th Hants
Pte E. Roland Budd	2nd 4th Hants
Lieut E. Maurice B. Cambie	9th K.O.Y.L.I.
Rflm Alfred Darvill	51st London
Spr William Eastment	4th Canadian E.
1st Cl Po James H. Edney	H.M.S. *Laurentic*
Pte Maurice T. Gardner	3rd West Yorks.
Gnr J. Rotchford George	R.F.A.
Pte Ernest B. Harris	28th London
Bdr Francis J. Hurst	R.F.A.
Pte George Kelsey	R.E.
Pte Harry E. Kemp	2nd 5th Lincoln
Cpl Edward Marsh	10th Hants
Sergt Frank Martin	9th Rifle Brigade
Pte Fred Mitchell	3rd Hants.
Gnr Priddon Musgrave	R.F.A.
2nd Lieut Manfred V.J. Nash	25th London
Sto Po Harry Neale	H.M.S. *Invincible*
Sergt Albert C. Newnan	1st Rifle Brigade
Pte Harry Newnan	8th Royal Berks
Pte William C. Norgate	1st Notts & Derby
Pte Richard Norgate	1st D.C.L.I.
Pte Gordon E. J. Ovenden	2nd 6th Sussex
C.P.O. William Passingham	K.M. S. *Savage*
Pte Albert E. Petts	50th Canadian I.
AB William M. Poole	H.M.S. *Invincible*
Cpl William Privett	Queens R.W. Surrey
Spr Frederick G. Robinson	R.E.
Pte Ernest A. Simpson	14th Hants.
Pte Cecil S. Simpson	9th Devon
OS William E. Simpson	H.M.S. *Glory IV*

1st CL Sto Harry Smith	H.M.S. Submarine D.6.
Pte Stanley Tancock	2nd 5th Somerset L.I.
Pte John D. Tomlinson	48th Australian I.
Pte Stanley R. Wheeler	R.M.L.I.
Pte William G. Wickham	12th Canadian I.
Sergt Sidney Wilks	9th Rifle Brigade

World War 1939-45

Flt Lieut E. Gordon Brettle, D.F.C.	R.A.F.Y.R.
Lieut Oliver Carr R.N.	H.M.S. *Diamond*
Flt Lieut. E. William Court	R.A.F.
1st Class Stoker W.J Cox	H.M.S. *Argus*
Signalman Laurence R. Ford	Royal Corps of Signals
Private Charles A. Griffin, R.M.	H.M.S. *Hood*
Guardsman A. Stewart Guy	Scots Guards
Captain G. Geoffrey Hale	75th (Sy) Med.Regiment R.A.
L/Corporal Douglas B. Hall	Royal Engineers
Flying Officer Kenneth R. Hall	R.A.F.
Gunner Albert B. Henty	69th Regiment R.A.
Flt Lieut John C. Horlock	R.A.F.V.R.
Captain R. A. H. Lawrence	1st Batt. Royal Fusiliers
1st Class Stoker Alfred F. Legg	H.M. Submarine *Trooper*
Captain M. K. Minards, M.C.	R.A.
Sergeant Navigator Morris J. Norgate	R.A.F.
Staff Sergeant Arthur T. Oates	R.A.O.C.
Flt Sergeant Ronald Watson	R.A.F.
L/Corporal Stanley S. Woodley	3rd Batt. Grenadier Guards

THE WINDOWS: Two fine stained glass windows adorn the church. The larger one over the altar was the gift of Mr Deacon in memory of his parents, who resided at Ropley Manor. The other window on the south wall was given by the vicar, Mr Geldart, in memory of his wife.

THE CHURCH CLOCK originally had only one face on the west wall of the tower and was dated 1726 and removed in the restoration of 1896. The present clock was installed to commemorate the coronation of Edward VII and was officially dedicated on October 28th 1903 when the vicar, W.H. Leak, gave an impressive sermon on the 'Value of Time'.

THE CHURCH PLATE: This is considered to be one of the finer collections of Elizabethan plate in the county. The beautiful fully ornamented chalice and paten-cover of silver were made in 1592 and could be described as a drinking cup. (Queen Elizabeth I is said to have ordered all chalices to be made into drinking cups.) The cup is unusually deep and widens at the lip. A pair of silver flagons have the inscription 'The gift of John Walling and Jane Andross to the Parish of Ropley, Hampshire, in memory of Mr William Andross, a pious and charitable inhabitant of the said parish, who died 17th April, 1714, aged 70 years'. A silver alms dish is inscribed, 'The gift of Jane Andross, late wife of Mr Andross in the parish church of Ropley, 1715'.

THE CHURCHYARD: This has been used for burials for centuries and in the older parts nearer the church there are some vaults. Miss Hagen generously gave two extensions, one in 1906 and the other in 1928, and more recently Jim Hale, of one of Ropley's oldest families, presented a further extension in 1980. A Garden of Rest is now available for cremations, and near the south porch there is a small Garden of Remembrance for tributes to the World War dead. An ancient yew faces the south porch, now aged and with its lower limbs supported. The Lych Gate at the upper entrance to the Churchyard was presented in August 1936 by Mr H. Geldart as a token of his twenty years' service in the parish. Over the past 20 years the care and maintenance of the churchyard has been in the hands of Colonel T.M. Walker (Churchwarden 1969-79) assisted by volunteers from the Church Garden Society, whose chairman, Churchwarden Patrick Tarabella, took over the responsibility in 1988.

THE CHURCH REGISTERS: 'In the name of God. Amen. By an Authoritie and Commission of the most excellent Prince Henrye, Kynge of England, and France etc...The injunction, September 5, 1538, that you and every parson, vicaire, and curate within this Diocese shall for every Churche, kepe one Boke or Registere, wherein you shall write the Date and yere of every Weddying, Christening, and Burying, made within your Parish for your tyme, and so everyman succeedying you likewise, and shall ther insert every Person's name that shall be so wedded, christened or burried.'

Such was the Act that gave authority to the order of Thomas Cromwell, Primate and Vice-Regent to King Henry VIII, so that our island story would be recorded in every parish for the benefit of all generations.

In 1597 it was ordered by the Convocation of Canterbury that parchment books should be provided for the registers and that transcripts be made on parchment from the existing registers on paper.

The date on the first page of Ropley Church Registers is 1537 and the first entries are dated 1538. The original books were rebound in two volumes in 1906 at the expense of Archdeacon Fearon and presented to the Church.

There are several gaps in the record, particularly in marriages from 1702 to 1755. From that date the record appears to be complete.

An Act of Parliament in 1668 and repealed in 1817 required that wool should be used for 'shroud, shirt or shift'. This Act was intended to advance the wool trade and registers during this period duly recorded 'burial in woolens' to confirm to the order. Other records used the term 'affidavit supplied'. In her *Annals of Old Ropley* Miss Hagen points to the many old Ropley names which have gone on from generation to generation—the Budds, Childs, Norgates, Privetts, Windebanks, Passinghams, Lambournes and Hales, some still with us—and on our War Memorials—today. One could also mention village names whose marks have been left on our roads and lanes—Dunsell, Hammond, Gascoigne, Berry, Webb, Brisland and others, some better known than others nowadays.

The Register is now kept in the County Records Office in Winchester.

ROPLEY VICARS: Continuity over the past four and a half centuries is shown as follows:

1538 Nicholas Symonson	1672 John London
1540 Thomas Gray	1711 Joseph Alexander
1544 John Gymmell	1724 Henry Cooper
1545 James Meyke	1746 P. Henvill
1545 John Venables	1757 William Howley Snr.
1552 Nicholas Alexander	1796 William Howley Jnr.

1565 Cuthbert Dickenson	(1813/28 Bishop of London)
1573 Edward Clive	1828/48 Archbishop of Canter-
	bury)
1598 Roger Hedges	1811 W. Evans
1622-3 John Lewman	1818 Samuel Maddock
	1871 Thomas Woodhouse

1882 Order in Council makes Ropley an independent parish.

1891 F. H. Baring	1937 Peter Were
1891 W. H. Leak	1954 John S. Berry
1912 H. S. Kelsey	1961 J. Arthur Hitchins
1915 S. R. Cambie	1967 Anthony V. Willmont
1916 H. W. C. Geldart	1977 Anthony Chambers
	1983 Alastair Dunn

The first available record of any personality among the above is that of William Howley, senior, who was inducted in 1757 and supervised many of the alterations in the Georgian church. It was he who was probably the first tenant of the Old Vicarage in Vicarage Lane (now 'Rook-wood'), although the stables and coach house were not built until 1891.

Apart from William Howley, junior, who became Archbishop of Canterbury (see IV), the best known man as incumbent of this parish was undoubtedly Samuel Maddock, several anecdotes of whom are contained in the *Annals of Old Ropley*. His long tenancy in the office was apparently not his only attribute, as he seems to have been quite a personality. His was a forthright character and his introduction to the parish was welcomed with mixed feelings which, in time, developed into a deep respect. His sermons were direct and to the point, couched in simple language, without any discrimination so that he was not popular with some members of his congregation and regularly persecuted by youths in the village. On one occasion a group of youths planned to attack his carriage as he came down the road from Monkwood but at the crucial moment a cloudburst foiled their plans. Simple country folk henceforth attributed divine powers to the vicar.

Mr Maddock once had an altercation with Mr Mulcock of Ropley Lodge, mainly due to the latter's illiteracy (he himself and his wife Anne were prolific writers), and the 'squire' never again attended the vicar's services. Mr Maddock's strong personality also affected a former reprobate William Faichen, to such an extent that Faichen eventually became master of the school later founded by the vicar (see X). Mr Maddock thoroughly condemned the wave of smuggling in the village, although there is no record of his ever having denounced any of his parishioners to the authorities. One of his brothers Robert, became a missionary in India where he died, and the new school was erected in his memory by the vicar and his family.

W.H. Leak came to Ropley after it became a separate parish. Previously he had been at Bishop's Sutton where he had organised the restoration of St Nicholas' Church. When he came to Ropley he found this church, too, in a bad state of repair and it was largely due to his efforts that the drastic restoration of 1896 was carried out.

H. Geldart was the incumbent at a critical period, for he became vicar during the transition from the staid Edwardian period, with all its regard for the establishment, into the modern era, and his guiding influence for twenty-one years was important for the village as we know it today. A scholarly and kindly man, he left a sum of money as an annual charity to the needy of the Parish, at his death.

Peter Were came to Ropley from St Luke in Maidenhead. He was a shy man, utterly devoted to his parishioners. It may be a token of his popularity that everyone in the parish always referred to him as 'Peter Were'. During the early days of his ministry he was a keen member of the Scout Movement, and just before he came to Ropley he had published his *Yarns at the Scouts Own'*. He was a clever ventriloquist and sometimes used his dummy at the children's services or in school to impress the point of his talks. He conducted an annual camp in the Isle of Wight for the choirboys and was always a favourite of the younger generation. For ten years he was an inspector of schools in the Winchester diocese and for a while was secretary of the Winchester Diocesan Clergy School. He was a regular contributor to the Hampshire Chronicle, to which he subscribed for thirty-five years. He left Ropley in 1954 and died in April 1973.

Ropley's last three vicars have all come from the Birmingham area, and two of them were from the world of business. Tony Willmont brought with him a breath of youthful ebullience, and it is perhaps largely due to him and his caring wife Lindy that St Peter's has such a lively following among the young of the Parish. Anthony Chambers came from a career in insurance and was a quieter man. He and his wife Fiona took a close interest in the choir and music of the church, which have prospered since then under the untiring leadership of Barbara Longlands, organist and Director of Music. Alastair Dunn was formerly a legal adviser to the British Petroleum Company in Iran, where he met his dedicated young wife Sheila, a missionary nurse in that country. Both have retained their long interest in missionary work while playing an active and hospitable role in the day to day affairs of the villages. It was in Tony Willmont's time that the village magazine, in more or less its present form, was born. Prior to 1972 the Parochial Church Council had distributed a simple leaflet-form newsletter which was hardly adequate. After discussions that year within the P.C.C. the new P.C.C. secretary Dr Norman Armstrong undertook the production and distribution of a much enlarged 'community magazine', naming it 'BIS MON ROP TIS' in 1977 when members of all four Parishes (Ropley, Monkwood, W. Tisted and Bishops Sutton) all became recipients free of charge. Norman and Sylvia Armstrong ran the magazine for 15 years with the help of voluntary distributors until forced to retire for health reasons in 1988. Their modest remuneration was regularly donated to Christian Aid, and in recognition of their long service the Ropley Society organised a presentation to them in January 1988. Since then the magazine has been competently run by a new arrival in the village from the U.S.A.—Bette Wilson.

The church finances have been in the safe hands of J.C. 'Mac' Macinness for the past quarter of a century. A former Senior Education Officer and District Commissioner of Scouts in Winchester and a lifelong Scout, his interest in the movement found expression in the 1960s (among other ways) in the provision of accommodation for Scouts and Guides in the former stables of the Coffee Room (see XI) For a number of years he has successfully organised 'village walks' on Boxing Day and in the summer, to the benefit of various local bodies. He is one of Ropley's familiar figures as he walks the length and breadth of the village with his little dog.

IV

THE ARCHBISHOP AND 'ARCHBISHOP'S COTTAGE'

Ropley may well be proud of its sons, quite a number of whom have achieved considerable success in their respective careers. William Howley, junior, who left the village to become Archbishop of Canterbury is Ropley's best known son.

William Howley, senior, became Vicar of Ropley in 1757; the office included the church at Bishop's Sutton. He married a girl from West Meon. Little is known of his wife except that she could neither read nor write and consequently was considered to be of peasant stock. Both he and his wife, with their daughter, are buried in St Peter's Church in Ropley.

The only son of this marriage, born in 1766, was put out to nurse, as was the custom in those days, and his first home was a thatched cottage facing the village pond and now known as 'Archbishop's Cottage'. Said to be the oldest building in the village, the cottage at that time lacked windows to the two bedrooms which were consequently very dark. These bedrooms were accessed by a crude form of ladder.

William Howley, junior, began his education at Winchester College where his execrable versifying won him the prize for English verse for two successive years before he went on to New College, Oxford. He returned to Ropley to follow his father as vicar in 1796. In 1802 he left to be inducted as Vicar of Andover, was installed as Canon of Christ Church, Oxford, in 1804 and in 1809 was appointed Regius Professor of Divinity. One of his Oxford pupils was the Prince of Orange, later to become King William II of Holland.

He was married in 1805 to Mary Francis, daughter of John Bell of Southampton, and shortly afterwards he became Vicar of Bradford Peveril in Dorset.

In 1813 he was made a member of the Privy Council and consecrated Bishop of London. The ceremony at Lambeth was attended by Queen Charlotte and members of the Royal Family. As Bishop of London he officiated at the christening of the infant Victoria, daughter of the Duke and Duchess of Kent.

The next royal occasion that he attended was the Coronation of the Regent as King George IV in 1820.

He was elevated to the Archbishopric of Canterbury in 1828 and in 1830 he placed the crown on the 'Sailor' King William IV. In June, 1837, the King died at Windsor and the archbishop made his historic journey to Kensington Palace where at 5 am the young Princess Victoria was roused from her bed to be informed of her succession as Queen. The archbishop not only crowned her as Queen but also married her to Prince Albert.

The 'Archbishop's Cottage' today

William Howley, junior, was essentially a high churchman with rigid Victorian views, who undertook his obligations in the House of Lords seriously, some would say too seriously in that he strongly opposed the reformist movement of the time, including the Reform Bill of 1832, and he played little part in the Oxford Movement of his time. His strict orthodoxy was also shown when he supported the unpopular (and unsuccessful) Bill in Parliament designed to facilitate the divorce of William IV from Queen Caroline, on the grounds that 'the King can do no wrong'. He was a benefactor of the Moberley Library at Winchester College and the Howley-Harrison Library at Canterbury, and died in 1848 leaving a fortune of £120,000.

V

MONKWOOD MISSION CHURCH

In 1936, in answer to a request from the vicar, H. Geldart, the Church Army sent a mission to tour the hamlets of the parish. In the first two weeks the response was disappointing, but on the third Sunday they received an enthusiastic welcome in Monkwood, where the only Sunday services available were in the Methodist Chapel nearby at Charlwood.

As a result it was decided that a mission church should be acquired for Monkwood, and Captain Hyde-Parker of Monkwood House gave a piece of land for the purpose. The Bishop of Winchester granted a license to hold Divine Service there, subject to three conditions:

1. That the mission must never be a liability to the Diocese.
2. That three trustees should be appointed, one of whom must be the Vicar of Ropley.
3. That the accounts should be audited annually.

The wooden church was built at Medstead, dismantled and erected on its present site on the Petersfield Road at Monkwood. The bell and pulpit came from an old mission at Four Marks, and in response to an appeal organised by Mrs Hyde-Parker a Missal Desk was presented by the Ladies of Vancouver and altar cloths from the Ladies of Windsor, while the kneelers and hassocks were handmade by the ladies of the congregation.

The Church was consecrated by the Bishop of Winchester (Dr Garbett) in August, 1936, and has since been supported by legacies and donations. It was restored in cedar wood in the 'sixties.

In January 1947 the property was conveyed to the Winchester Diocesan Board of Finance in trust for the Ropley Parochial Church Council, and is now held for general ecclesiastical purposes including use of the premises by the vicar for divine services at his discretion.

The Mission Church was supervised for many years by Lay Reader Mr Musgrove Buxton and his wife who ran a Sunday School there until her death in 1987. It has continued under the supervision of Mrs Jennifer Wyeth.

VI

THE METHODIST CHAPEL

By the end of the 19th century the cult of John Wesley had increased throughout Wessex more than any other nonconformist sect, and in Ropley it seems to have been the only one to have had any following. The Methodist chapel was some distance from the village centre, at the junction of Gilbert Street and Andrews Lane, at that time called Chapel Lane. A footpath existed across the fields from the village pond. The pastor at this time was A. Lowe.

During the summer months Gospel Tent meetings were held in Hammonds Lane, in the recreation ground and by the village pond. The most enthusiastic members of the local congregation were Mr J. Miller and Mr J. Goodall, who led a movement towards the erection of a new chapel. In about eighteen months the local congregation had raised a sum of £200, and the new building was erected in Vicarage Lane opposite the recreation ground at a cost of £600. It was opened on 21st January, 1909, by Miss Scott, sister of the Rev G. Scott of Winchester. The active membership of the Primitive Methodist Church in Ropley was little more than thirty, none of whom could be considered wealthy.

The old chapel was sold and converted into a private house, now known as Elinor House. Another chapel existed at Charlwood but its congregation gradually dwindled and it became derelict and was demolished.

After the Second World War it was doubtful if the chapel in Vicarage Lane could pay its way, but the efforts of its small following kept it alive. A youth club was formed to bolster social activities and provide something towards its finances. At this time there was a general movement towards co-operation between the Methodists and the Church of England, and exchange visits were sometimes made on Sundays. The Ecumenical Movement eased the problems of the small Methodist congregation and it decided to sell the chapel. This was done, and its site is now occupied by a new dwelling house and the congregation was absorbed into that of the Parish Church.

VII

COMMUNICATIONS

(a) The Roads

The Romans left us a legacy of a fine road system which the Saxons and Normans allowed to deteriorate.

It was not until the wheel was developed to the stage where it was adapted for the carriage of passengers that the need for sound carriageways was realised. In the 17th century a journey by coach was a hazardous adventure, requiring a hardy constitution to survive it. In those days it was not unusual for a journey from Portsmouth to London to take as long as four days.

In 1712 a route from London to Southampton existed coming by way of Bagshot and Farnham, then into Hampshire to Alton. From there the road continued on to Bighton, Old Alresford and thence by Sewards Bridge to Longwood Down, Morestead, Twyford and Bishopstoke. This road bypassed Ropley completely.

Maintenance was unevenly shared between landowners and parishes but was widely neglected and conditions became so bad that, after suffering numerous disasters to their vehicles, coach owners collectively appealed to Parliament for something to be done.

'An Act for repairing and widening the roads leading from a place called Basingstone, near the town of Bagshot, in the parish of Windlesham, in the County of Surrey, through Frimley, and Farnham in the same county; and from thence through Bentley, Hollyborn, Alton, Chawton, Ropley, New Alresford and Mattingley, otherwise Matterley Lane, to the City of Winchester in the County of Southampton.'

This was the full title of the Act of Parliament authorising a new road in 1753 during the reign of George II. This Act was further amended in 1768 and at intervals of several years after that.

Work started in 1753 and this was the beginning of the system of toll roads and turnpikes. In the Curtis Museum at Alton may be seen the board depicting the charges for using the turnpike roads. These charges were collected at toll gates long since abolished, but the toll houses, conspicuous for their octagonal ground plan and conical roofs may still be identified on the Selborne Road and elsewhere. In some parts of the country, particulaly in South Wales, there was great opposition to the charges in the form of attacks on the toll gates.

The Act also named trustees responsible for the expenditure of the money collected by tolls, money to be used for the maintenance of the roads. The greater number of nominees were clergymen, following the precedence of ecclesiastical responsibility for bridges. In 1834, before the railways offered a challenge, the amount of money taken at the tolls of Hampshire was £28,035, with half of this going back into the roads. That worked out at £23 a mile. The peak was in 1837 when the price went up to £25 a mile. When the railways came into the picture, the expenditure on the roads dropped quickly until in 1870 it was only £10 a mile. 'Everybody thought the day of the roads was finished. This period of complete neglect led to the things we are suffering from today, such as bad foundations', said the county surveyor in 1953.

The Local Government Act of 1929 gave responsibility for the upkeep of the roads to the County Councils, with the exception of unclassified roads in urban districts. Parallel to that was a state aid scheme especially with regard to trunk roads.

The War in 1939 prevented any proper modernisation of the roads passing through Ropley and after the cessation of hostilities the question of road improvements had to take second place to more urgent requirements.

Meanwhile traffic speeds were increasing and so was the number of accidents, notably on the bending road east of the Chequers Inn. In a speech given by the County Surveyor, Brigadier A.C. Hughes, in 1953, on the 'Development of the Hampshire Road System', he said, 'The present day roads were very little different from those of the old Roman system of over a thousand years ago. The Roman efforts at road-building were very good despite the lack of control afterwards.'

Shortly afterwards began a reconstruction programme, not only for the A31, but generally for the whole county, and the alignment was improved at the Dean to allow more visibility throughout its length. These improvements were extended to widening the carriageway to 24 feet and the inclusion of footpaths on one side or other of the road from Bishop's Sutton to North Street. The junction of the Petersfield Road at the Anchor Inn was also reconstructed and an obstructive stone wall at Ropley Lodge Cottage was removed The original roadway may still be seen opposite Gascoigne Lane.

(b) Road Transport

In the last century villagers usually kept within the parish boundaries except on special occasions such as fair days or the sheep fairs at Alresford or Alton when they would make the journey on a wagon or horse brake (wagonette) or on foot. Such walks were undertaken, even by children, as a matter of course and were not considered to be at all unusual. Footpaths criss-crossed the parish and 45 of these are still in use. Stiles and signs are nowadays maintained by the East Hants District Council and the routes—most of them originally the product of day-by-day use of villagers on foot—are now extensively used for leisure as well as practical purposes, in spite of difficulties encountered through ploughing-over and growing crops.

But with road improvements came omnibus services, and by the 1930s The Aldershot and District Traction Company were operating a route from Aldershot to Winchester via the A31 road. This daily service was an hourly one in each direction. The fare stage was from the Windmill Inn to the Anchor Inn. Compulsory stops provided with shelters were sited at the Anchor and Chequers Inns, but there were also request stops at the Ropley Motor Works, Berry Hill, North Street and the Shant. In 1970 the Traction Company amalgamated with the Thames Valley Omnibus Company, the new combination becoming the Alder Valley Omnibus Company and one of the largest independent companies in the country. The familiar green and cream livery of the Aldershot company was changed to red and cream.

Also between the Wars the Little Wonder Bus Company of Petersfield began to operate a bus service three days a week from Petersfield Market to the Anchor Inn. This was a family business which was well supported as the route included West Tisted, Privett and Froxfield.

After the War, in 1946, the Little Wonder Company extended their service to Alresford daily, in competition with the Traction Company. They also introduced a special service on Tuesdays (Alton market days) and Saturdays from Petersfield to Alton, via Froxfield, Privett, Stapley Lane, Petersfield Road to Maddocks Hill, then to Church Street and

Gilbert Street, Four Marks and Farringdon. This was a route never before covered by a bus company.

But with the growth of private car ownership support declined and the Little Wonder Bus Company reverted to a three-day-a-week service to Alresford, and eventually sold out to the Liss Omnibus Company at Bordon. The Liss Omnibus Company soon realised that the Alresford route was no longer a paying concern and discontinued the service. There is now no public transport available from the Anchor Inn to Monkwood or Tisted. Voluntary and occasional services provide shopping links from Ropley to Petersfield, Alresford and Alton.

(c) The 'Watercress Line'—Mid-Hants Railway

Today's 'Watercress Line' dates back to 1861 when the Alton Alresford and Winchester Railway Ltd was formed with an authorised capital of £150,000. Gangs of Irish labourers or 'navigators' worked on the cuttings and banks for four years, and when the through line from Alton to Winchester was opened on 2nd October 1865 it had stations at Ropley, Alresford and Itchen Abbas. Medstead station was opened in 1868. The result was to link up the London and South Western Railway's line from London to Alton with the Winchester-Southampton route, and all the new stations were built with passing loops in anticipation of a busy through service. The L.S.W.R. operated the railway from the start and bought the line outright in 1884. It then settled down to a steady existence and became a valuable route for conveying military equipment to the southern ports during the Boer War and the first World War. New Alresford became the principal station thanks largely to the daily consignments of watercress to London, while Ropley was the first station on the long haul 'over the Alps' (as was said locally) to the 'summit' at Four Marks. Ropley station was staffed by a station master, booking clerk, two signalmen and two or three porters and looked more or less as it does today, with a siding for water and coal bunkers. It gained a high reputation for its attractive greenery and especially its topiary.

The line became part of the Southern Railway, along with the rest of the L.S.W.R., in 1923, and its decline started around 1930 with the spread of motor vehicles. Through trains to and from Southampton no longer used it, the passing loops were taken out at Ropley and Itchen

Abbas, and the service became a rural branch line between Alton, Winchester and Southampton, run by push-and-pull trains and operated by small tank engines.

Ropley Station about 1930

During the Second World War the Mid-Hants line was again in use in connection with the war effort, and Ropley station often reverberated to the rumble of troop and ammunition trains drawn by the huge 'Utility' 0-6-2 engines. It fortunately escaped the bombing raids, though a stick of bombs from a Messerschmidt just missed the line near North Street Farm in February 1943.

After the War the pre-war pattern was resumed, with about seven trains a day operating. In 1948 it was nationalised under British Rail, but the slow decline continued. Efforts were made to improve the service in 1957 with the introduction of an hourly service of diesel trains serving the commuter trains from Alton. But at Ropley the station master disappeared and staff were reduced; and following the Beeching Report of 1963 Ropley became an unstaffed halt. (Walter Woodley, who had worked on the line for 35 years and was responsible for the topiary of the old yew trees among other things, was detailed as a guard-conductor, collecting the fares between Alresford and Alton).

Notice of closure of the line was announced in 1968, evoking a strong public protest organised by local councils and the public under the leadership of Mr John Taylor of Winchester Rural District Council, supported by Mr A.E. Guy of Ropley Parish Council and many others. After a series of public enquiries, postponements and much acrimony, the last train ran on 4th February 1973.

Meanwhile, the first steps towards preservation of the line had been taken, and the Ombudsman's report published after the closure in August 1973, had suggested that British Rail's calculations were wrong and that the line was an economic proposition.

The Winchester and Alton Railway Company (now the Mid-Hants Railway PLC) was formed in May 1973, supported by the Mid-Hants Railway Preservation Society, and funds were raised through share issues in 1975 to establish a preserved steam service between Alton and Alresford. Intensive activity followed in 1976 when the track was laid between Alresford and Ropley, station buildings were restored, signalling equipment installed and the passing loop at Ropley relaid. Staff were trained, carriages refurbished and the all important steam locomotives brought into use. The Alresford-Ropley first section of the line was opened by the Chairman of the Hampshire County Council on 30th April 1977.

The next aim was to extend the line to Alton to link up with British Rail services to and from Waterloo, and the relaying of track from Ropley to Medstead and Four Marks was accomplished between May 1982 and January 1983—entirely through enthusiastic volunteers. Meanwhile more steam locomotives and carriages had been acquired and restored, the locomotive shed at Ropley completed, and the first train ran from Ropley into the refurbished station at Medstead and Four Marks on 28th May 1983.

A further heavy task of track laying between Four Marks and Alton then followed in difficult weather conditions, and the first Mid-Hants train ran into Alton on 25th May 1985, completing the Alresford-Alton line and signalling the accomplishment of a mammoth job in a remarkably short period of time with limited resources.

The above can only be a brief outline of the 'Watercress Line's' remarkable success story since 1973. Ropley has had its full share in the success (e.g. award of the Best Preserved Station presented to Ropley Station by the Chairman of British Rail, Sir Peter Parker, in 1982) and has played its full part in the numerous celebrations and enterprises launched by the company over a short period since 1973. The Railway carried its one-millionth passenger in December 1988 and is now recognised as not only a major tourist attraction, but also a useful service in its own right.

An anniversary celebration was held in Ropley on 1-2 July 1989 to commemorate the opening of the main line from London to Southampton in 1839.

(d) The Post

The Royal Mail as we now know it was founded in the 17th century in the time of Charles II, under a postmaster general. It is recorded that at about this time it cost Daniel Defoe twopence to send a letter a distance of eighty miles. Mails were then only carried on selected 'post' roads, one being from London to Edinburgh. In those early days the mounted courier service delivered letters to a 'post office' usually a hostelry, where the local carrier took them on his rounds to the local villages, together with goods to supply the village shops. As a carrier could only visit a village once a week or fortnight, this visit was usually an eagerly awaited event, not only due to the collection of goods and the mail but because it was often the only source of news from the outside world.

In time the courier service was replaced by stage coaches which usually travelled a stage of twelve to fifteen miles from one coaching hostel to the next. In 1767, after one of the three big fires that almost destroyed the town of New Alresford, the Bell Inn was built on the site of the old market inn. Here the coach from Southampton stopped to change horses and any mail was delivered or collected. The next stage was the Swan Hotel in the High Street at Alton. Until the erection of the Dean Filling Station there had been a coach house and stables at the Anchor Inn, but these were demolished to make way for the present car park.

In an extract from the *The Universal British Directory of 1792* the mail coach from London to Poole is described as passing through Alresford every morning between 3 and 4 am. Its return was timed for 11 pm. The Post House opened at 8 am and closed at 9 pm.

A mail cart plied regularly between Alton and Winchester and villagers used to set their time by the moment it passed the Chequers

Inn at Ropley. Very few pillar boxes existed in the early part of the last century and the driver in his horse-drawn mail cart, after collecting mail at Ropley Post Office (now the Old Post House in Church Street), drove down to the Petersfield Road on the way to Alresford. By 1851 a post office was established in South Street, Ropley, and as the outlying hamlets developed two more post offices were opened at the Dean and at Monkwood. The penny post, which had originally been confined to London, was extended to cover the rest of the country in 1840.

During this century there have been several changes in the location of the village post office. From Church Street, where it occupied three different sites, it moved to Hammonds Lane, next door to the Star Inn, and was in the charge of Mr Le Pateurel. The next move was in the 1950s to a site in Church Lane with Mr L. Shier as postmaster; but nowadays the sole postal service is at the Dean (Mr John Wyatt) with deliveries made direct to the village from Alresford.

VIII

THE PILGRIMS' WAY

The route of the Pilgrims' Way from Winchester to Canterbury has always been an interesting subject about which there is a great diversity of opinion.

In Chaucer's day there was of course no road system as there is today, and transport was by horse, ass, cart or on foot. Even carriages did not exist. From earliest times long journeys were made over ridgeways, or people followed cattle droves or narrow bridleways or footpaths. These were created by continual passage over the years across otherwise virgin ground.

In *Pilgrimage to Canterbury* by Henry Fearon the author describes a route from Winchester via the Worthies to Old Alresford Wield and Medstead to Alton. On this road one would probably call in for sanctuary and refreshment at the Chapel at Godsfield near Lanham where there was a Chapel of Ease maintained by the Knights Hospitaliers of St John. This chapel has in recent times been used as a grain store on Godsfield Farm, but it still retains its original form with an apse, lancet windows and original low-arched doorway. Another chapel still exists in use at North Baddesley. This was originally built for the Knights Templars but was later taken over by the Knights of St John, who still hold the deeds.

Other writers, notably Hilaire Belloc, describe a route through Ropley, and in his book *The Old Road* (quoted at some length in Marianne Hagen's book *Annals of Old Ropley*) Belloc says 'archeological discoveries mark the whole road'. Belloc's route goes by way of Whitehill to Bishop's Sutton, then by way of the Dean to the Anchor Inn at Ropley, then follows Hook Lane, across the grounds of Ropley House, behind the Chequers Inn, to Brislands Lane by the Manor Farm House. There we follow Belloc's route to Four Marks, where at the junction with Lymington Bottom stands a cottage that used to bear the name of 'Pilgrims' (later renamed Keepsake Cottage). Brislands Lane was until recently still known by some of the older residents as the Pilgrims' Way. The Way then followed Blackberry Lane towards Chawton.

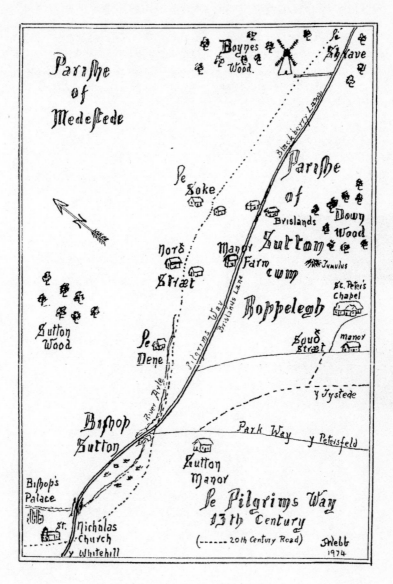

The Pilgrims' Way
(map by J.A.L. Webb)

But the Ropley route, if indeed it was a pilgrims' route, must surely be only one of many and the probable conclusion is that there never was any definitive Pilgrims' Way as such. Pilgrims would use tracks and routes already in existence; and just as present day hikers plan their journey from day to day, so it seems did those pilgrims dependent upon the vagaries of the weather and rumours they would hear of footpads and other hazards on the way.

IX

SMUGGLING

As you approach the harbour on the main street in Polperro, Cornwall, you are invited to descend some steps on your right, to enter into the depths and times of the Smugglers' Cellars. Here, carefully preserved in the original cellars, is the evidence of smuggling through the ages, from the 17th century to the Ulster troubles of the 1970s. The exhibition is not confined to Cornish smuggling, which has a world-wide reputation, but also includes exhibits, charts and maps from Hampshire and Sussex.

Among the exhibits are charts, pictures and other articles from Bosham in Chichester Harbour, Emsworth, Langstone and Farlington. It was from sources such as these, and from Titchfield on the Meon River, that the men of Ropley and the neighbourhood obtained their illicit supplies.

In the 18th century smuggling was rife throughout Hampshire. Then for a period the practice became almost extinct, only to be revived more intensively in the next century. The heavy duties demanded by successive governments to help in paying off the national debt incurred through the French wars turned the illicit distribution of dutiable merchandise into a widespread 'black market'.

The goods were collected from the places already mentioned and transported by cart or pack horse, usually at night, into the hinterland 'as far north as Ropley', to quote from T.W. Shore's *The History of Hampshire*. This is not quite true because we know that smuggled goods were sometimes hidden in the church tower at Medstead, and Goatacre near the same village has its own tales to tell. Smuggling extended even further to Herriard Park and the little church of Nateley Scures. But the real centre of the 19th century smuggling in Hampshire was in Ropley, where villagers and gentry combined to defeat the investigations of the excise officers.

As you proceed along the C18 towards Petersfield just beyond Lyewood House, a narrow lane descends sharp right into a gorge while the Petersfield Road continues up the hill. The lane climbs again up from the bottom to the crossroads at Merryfield. This is Smugglers' Lane and at its bottom is a white-walled house called 'Smugglers'.

Nowadays the foliage is kept under control and daylight penetrates to make this a beautiful picture, but a century ago the overhanging greenery gave a sinister air to the scene, as if to ward off inquisitive visitors.

In Hampshire the word 'moonshine' was a name given to smuggled spirits as well as to the products of illicit stills, and it was said that at the beerhouse that is now 'Smugglers' an honest visitor could buy a legal beer in the front while a local quaffed 'moonshine' at the back.

There were goods other than spirits and wines, chief of which were lace, silks and jewellery. The silks were reasonably easy to transport and store in bolts. The liquids were usually in small barrels called 'tubs' These were hidden in some unusual places. A dung heap where the Bighton road joined the Alresford road was one such hide until it was discovered. Near West Tisted was a 'nest with 40 eggs in it', which translated meant a dell with 40 tubs at the bottom.

Most of the houses and cottages in Ropley had their caches of illicit goods, and the villagers and gentry were both involved in the industry. The goods were hidden in cellars, woods, behind high hedges and even in the tithe barn of the Old Parsonage.

On Sunday evenings after the evening service in St Peter's the villagers would flock to Monkwood where the smuggled goods were displayed for sale and the place had an atmosphere 'like a Fair'.

In 1928 while making an extension to his dining room at Ryecroft (now Ropley Grove), Admiral Henderson discovered a chamber about seven feet deep and seven feet square. The finding of this cellar revived a story about Major Lavender, the squire who used to live there. He was a J.P., a churchwarden, a member of the Hunt, and also a leading smuggler. Towards the end of the 18th century excise officers arrived to ask the squire to sign a warrant for permission to search the 'Smugglers' cottage at Monkwood. The squire was in no doubt that the contraband was in the cottage. As it was close to noon he invited the officers to dinner and while arranging the meal he sent his groom to the cottage to get rid of the 'stuff'. After an exceedingly good meal and the warrant duly signed, the officers duly departed on a fruitless errand. The 'stuff' had been safely lowered to the bottom of a 200-foot well, to be recovered after the unwelcome visit. Little did the excise officers know of the cache they were so close to as the squire signed the warrant. The well is still to be seen at 'Smugglers'.

In her book, *Annals of Old Ropley*, Miss M.S. Hagen relates the above and other stories of smuggling days in Ropley. It appears that Ropley House was also involved in the smuggling. This house was built upon the foundation of a much older house, and during alterations to the house in the 19th century it was said a flight of steps was discovered 'leading down no one knew where'.

It was said that the young Mr Duthy of Ropley House was connected with the smugglers and used to take his father's horses from the stables at night to help them. When Captain Duthy learnt of this he ordered his son out of the house; but his sisters helped him out with money and other things which they let down to him at night from their bedroom window.

Another story is that of the redoubtable Henry Prior who lived at Monkwood. He collected a cart load of whiskey 'tubs' at Portsmouth, but the Custom House got wind of it, and he found himself being pursued. Not to be outdone he put his horse into a gallop and maintained that gait all the 30 miles to Ropley, eluding his pursuers and arriving safely with his load intact.

The Rev Maddock, Vicar of Ropley, strongly and openly denounced this popular local sport of smuggling. It is remarkable that he retained his hold on the village in spite of his unpopular stand.

X

THE SCHOOL

Before 1826 no school existed in the parish, and it was the Rev Samuel Maddock, vicar at the time, who founded the first day school which opened on 6th May that year in a small house on the present Petersfield Road, with one William Faichen as teacher in charge.

The circumstances of the school's early days are described in a pamphlet called *Annals of a Village Schoolmaster,* written by Mrs Maddock, the vicar's wife. It appears that William Faichen had been brought up in a public house in Medstead where his publican father was an unsavoury character. The boy went to work at the age of 12 in public houses in Winchester and in Portsmouth, from whence he ran away back to Bighton where he was befriended by the rector. He appears to have become a drunkard and a 'miserable sinner' by that time; but he married and went to work in a carriage works near the Ship Inn at Bishop's Sutton, where he met Mr Maddock. His whole life and character were reformed through this friendship and he devoted himself to teaching local children on his spare evenings in the belfry of St Nicholas church. Mr Maddock meanwhile became fired with the idea of founding a day school at Ropley for the children of Ropley and Bishop's Sutton, and when a school house was built on the Petersfield Road, Faichen was the obvious choice to run it. He remained until his untimely death four years later. He was buried in Bishop's Sutton church on 8th January 1830 and his funeral was attended by an impressive crowd of pupils and parents.

In May 1869 the original school house was replaced by a new building on the present day site built by the Maddock family in memory of a brother of the Samuel Maddock (Robert Maddock) who died a missionary in India. A monogram bearing his initials R.N.M. has been retained on the wall of the school today. The original school building on the Petersfield Road was destroyed by fire in 1976.

The new school was originally designed for about 100 children, and it was run at first by a series of mistresses, assisted by a pupil teacher. Average attendance was between 50 and 80 children (aged three to 13) taught in one large classroom. In 1884 an additional infant teacher was appointed. Lessons comprised the three 'R's drill, singing and needle-work, and the vicar came regularly to give scripture lessons. Attendance was not compulsory and children stayed away for all sorts of reasons (haymaking, hop-picking etc.) On one day more than half the children were absent 'the parents not daring to send them whilst the east wind lasts', and epidemics took their toll.

In the spring of 1887 Frederick Rice became Headmaster and made significant improvements. The average weekly attendance went up to 125. Fees were set at 2d a family a week when two or more children attended (1d for only one) and a School Attendance Officer was called in to investigate absenteeism. A spacious new schoolroom was added in 1888 to cope with an influx, and by 1892 there were 139 children in all on the roll and an additional assistant mistress was taken on.

In 1892 Mr Rice was succeeded by Mr R.C. Turner, who stayed for 38 years and with Mrs Turner and Miss Capp supporting him, this was a time of great stability. Numbers on the register rose to 170 in the 1890s, but fell back to 135 by 1926. Mr Turner developed the curriculum considerably and opened a school museum and library. He was a man of considerable ability and integrity who was not only the village schoolmaster but active in many phases of village life. Among his many honorary jobs were those of choirmaster and organist, chairman of the Parish Council, secretary of the Cricket Club and other bodies. During his headmastership a classroom on the west side was added.

Mr Turner retired in 1930 and in the remaining years before the school became a Junior Mixed and Infants School in 1938 a scheme for hot mid-day dinners was introduced. In January 1939 Miss Muriel Slinn took over as Headmistress and saw the school through most of the war years, when the school had to cope with evacuees and evacuated teachers from London.

In September 1947 Miss Gladys Proctor became headmistress and remained at Ropley for 20 years, a period of much change and improvement. By 1950 there were now 120 pupils taught in four classes in three classrooms, many of the children coming from Four Marks. An H.M. Inspectorate report of that year commented on the inadequate playground and inadequate water supply and the fact that the children had to use the Recreation Ground for games and the Village Hall for dinners and lessons. Bucket sanitation was still in use, and one wash hand basin served the entire school. But the inspectors felt that any improvements would have to await a final discussion on the status of the school under the 1944 Education Act, under which Church of England schools such as Ropley had the choice of being 'aided' or 'controlled'.

In 1952 it was decided that the school should remain 'aided' under the Diocese of Winchester, with Ropley Parochial Church Council required to find an annual quota towards its upkeep. But in view of the poor conditions and difficulty of finding funds for improvements, a meeting of the village called by the P.C.C. in 1955 reversed the earlier decision and the school became 'controlled' in 1956, with the County Council taking responsibility for its maintenance and the management shared between the P.C.C., the County Council and the Parish Council.

Plans then went ahead immediately to enlarge and modernise the buildings. By 1960 virtually a new school had been created for a total cost of about £20,000, and overcrowding had diminished with lower intake from Four Marks. The new construction included an assembly hall, fully equipped kitchen, three new classrooms, new toilets and office space and enlarged playing grounds and football pitch.

At the end of 1965 Miss Proctor retired to live in Alresford. She had presided with great dignity over a difficult period in the school's history.

Miss Proctor's successor was Mr Raymond Wardle who became headmaster in January 1966. By now the number of pupils had been reduced to manageable proportions, and the 82 pupils were taught in the three new classrooms and in the open area off the hall of the original building. During the three years of Mr Wardle's headship pupil numbers grew again to 118. In his last year as headmaster, the centenary of the old school building was marked by a special ceremony.

January 1970 saw the start of 16 years of expansion under the headship of Mr John Potter. This was a period of change: a broader curriculum, the encouragement of parental interest and involvement, and an emphasis on good academic standards. Also the school became increasingly involved in village life, with carol singing, street performances of a mummers play for St George's Day, and visiting the elderly. Traditional activities such as folk-singing and dancing were revived, links were forged between the church and the school, and regular performances of handbell ringing were given in both buildings.

52

As the numbers in the school increased the County Council provided a 'temporary' classroom at the side of the main building in April 1972, but the school continued to attract numbers of children from outside the catchment area and once again more space was needed. Parents and local residents raised money to build a swimming pool in 1973 and a further temporary classroom in 1977. A Friends of Ropley School Association was formed in 1980.

A highlight of the school's history occurred in 1976 with the 150 years' anniversary of the founding of the school. The village enjoyed a re-enactment of Samuel Maddock and William Faichen's struggle to start the school, performed outside the original thatched schoolhouse (which was sadly destroyed by fire six months later) and around the grave of Faichen in Bishop's Sutton Churchyard. Children from the school still place flowers on this grave each May following the Founders Day service in St Peter's Church. In 1977 school colours of brown, blue and gold were adopted for a school uniform and Mr Tony Gilliam designed a school badge in these colours, incorporating in the design two symbols of the school's founders—a cross and a wheel.

With the arrival of Mr Duncan Sergeant as headmaster in September 1986 the school moved into the technological age, and once again parents and local residents became involved in raising funds for the construction of a Library and Resources Room in 1989, by which time the numbers of pupils was around 160.

XI

THE COFFEE ROOM

The Coffee Room is situated in Church Street not far from the Church. It formed part of a larger property bought by Miss Hagen of Ropley House, who built it and dedicated it to the parish in memory of her parents.

It was opened on Monday 6th October 1883 by the vicar, the Thomas Woodhouse, assisted by the Rev A. Stogdon of Barton Lacey. Situated in the centre of the village, the room met a great need at the time as a meeting place. Miss Hagen organised regular meetings there of the Mothers' Union and of the Band of Hope, but it was her main intention that the room should be a meeting-place for the men of the parish, as an alternative to the ale-houses.

Among the most popular meetings were the Pleasant Sunday Afternoons, personally conducted by Miss Hagen, and characterised by hearty hymn singing. During the week, the room became a men's club, and when a troop of Boy Scouts was formed in 1906, it became their headquarters.

On Miss Hagen's death in 1932, she bequeathed the Coffee Room, together with the adjacent house 'Meadowside' (which had latterly become her home) and the adjoining stables and paddock, to the Winchester Diocese; the Deed of Trust drawn up in 1934 stressed that the primary use of the room was as a club for working men and boys of Ropley, and secondarily for Sunday School Bible Classes and other religious purposes, and for meetings (except party political meetings), and finally anything for the benefit of the Parish of Ropley. So far as the club was concerned, gambling, swearing and drinking were forbidden by its rules; the aim was 'to encourage honesty, sobriety and kindliness'.

In due course rentals from the house, paddock and stables, and income from the bequest, proved inadequate to maintain the Coffee Room, and in 1956 the house was sold to a private buyer, and the paddock to the County Education Authority to form part of the present school's playing field. Early in 1957, a proposal to sell the Coffee Room to the owner of Meadowside and rebuild on the site of the stables met with disapproval at a public parish meeting called by the Parish Council and attended by the trustees. Instead, the trustees decided to retain the Coffee Room as it was, to modernise it and to retain the stables. This was carried out, and a substantial cash gift from the district nurse (Miss Johnson—see XVIII) enabled the management committee to install new toilet facilities. The Coffee Room thus became once more a pleasant place for meetings.

The stables eventually became vacant, and in 1968 they were converted into a single hall and leased to the Scouts, Guides, Cubs and Brownies for use as a meeting-place and headquarters; the remaining buildings were let as garages and a store. The Guides and others have since materially helped with the maintenance of the Room.

The centenary celebrations were held in September 1983, attended by Mr Gerald Stogdon, great-nephew of the Rev Stogdon who assisted at the opening in 1883.

The Coffee Rooms are the responsibility of a management committee appointed by the Parochial Church Council; the committee may make provisions as to conditions of hiring, and the consumption of alcohol may be permitted on certain occasions. The Room is particularly popular for birthday parties, meetings, youth club activities and whist drives; it is a great asset to the village.

XII

PARISH HALL

During the nineteenth century, in common with most country villages, social entertainments usually took place in the village school. The new Coffee Room, opened in 1883, served a social need, but its limited space and confining rules was not always suitable for some meetings. In those days the entertainment consisted usually of concerts, socials and political meetings.

In December 1907 a meeting of residents was called and a committee, under the chairmanship of Mr H. Gisborne Holt of Grove Farm, was formed to raise funds for a village hall. This committee organised various functions such as jumble sales and fetes, and Lady Blackett of Ropley Grove directed a ladies' working party. There were no facilities available to hold dances or other large indoor functions, so most of the funds were raised through garden parties, fetes or sales of work.

By the outbreak of World War I in 1914 nearly £400 had been raised in seven years With the return to peace in 1918, an ex-Y.M.C.A. wooden hut was purchased and erected on a piece of land in Vicarage Lane, given by Major C. Holroyd of Ropley Manor, opposite what is now the ROMPS Children's Playground. This second-hand wooden building did indeed serve its purpose but it was unsightly, of a limited life and in constant need of maintenance and repair. The hall accounts were often overdrawn. The trusteeship was vested in the vicar and one other (not in the Parish Council) and doubts were felt in some quarters over the legal position concerning the hall.

The building served its purpose for a while, but by 1936 it had become obvious that a decision would have to be taken concerning its future. A public meeting was convened with the vicar, Mr H. Geldart, in the chair and a building committee was elected, led by Dr Gillies and Mr A.E. Guy, Secretary of the Parish Council. A site was selected to erect a new hall on the south-west corner of the Recreation Ground. This caused some trouble when it was found this was not permissible under an Act of Parliament governing such Recreation Grounds, unless an equal area of ground was added to the Recreation Ground. Sir Alan Horne of Ropley Manor then purchased an acre of ground on the west side of the ground and presented it to the parish, adding a generous cash contribution. The option on the site was now fully assured.

The architects designs and the specifications were greatly influenced by Government inspired recommendations for civil defence in the inter-war years. The final plans received high commendations from official quarters and were displayed at various exhibitions as an out-standing example of a modern village hall. The National Council of Social Services gave a grant towards the building costs and also loaned a sum of £500. The hall was built by H. Crispe and Son of Medstead and was officially opened by the Member of Parliament for the Petersfield Division, Sir Reginald Dorman-Smith MP on the 11th September, 1938.

With the object of providing funds to pay off the loan a Ladies Working Party was organised by Mrs Guy and others and soon earned a reputation under the title of 'The Busy Bees'. Various social functions were organised and the former Flower Show was revived in 1939 from which half the profits were handed to the hall funds.

Previously, in the old wooden hut, a series of 'sixpenny hops' were held on Saturday nights and after the opening of the new hall the 'hops' became 'shilling hops', also every Saturday. These dances proved to be very popular and after a short interruption on the outbreak of war they were resumed by the 'Busy Bees' in September 1940 and supported by mid-week whist drives. In 1942 Roy Vincent was able to form a band which played regularly until long after hostilities had ceased. During the war period the whole district was full of allied troops, mainly Americans and Canadians, and the hall was the head-quarters of the Home Guard, (headed by Colonel H. Strong) so the Saturday night dances were always crowded.

The revenue from these social events, run mainly by the 'Busy Bees' not only paid off the building debt, but also provided donations to the British Red Cross Society and other national wartime charities; and after the war their efforts continued to bring in a revenue of about £500 a year. Heating, mains water and improved drainage were installed and the finances were healthy.

With the introduction of rock-and-roll and jive, with entirely new types of music and dancing, attendance at the regular dances began to flag, and named bands were contracted with emphasis on a revival of 'old time' events and higher admission fees to meet the increased band charges. These dances often proved uneconomical as they catered not only for a different level of customer, but only a limited following of enthusiasts. Meanwhile, with a large inflow from Four Marks, the accommodation at Ropley School had become inadequate and the Hampshire County Council arranged by the early 50s for school meals, and later classes, to be held in the hall. These hirings brought in much needed income and helped to maintain the funds in a healthy condition.

The 'Busy Bees' had accumulated a balance of over £600 which paid for modernisation and enlargement to the kitchen. With a credit balance and assistance from the Hampshire Branch of the National Council of Social Services and the Ministry of Education, an additional room was built on to the original structure.

Following hard wear and tear of the years, the deal floor in the main hall had become worn and unserviceable in the late 1940s. After difficult negotiations by Mr A.E. Guy, the Ministry of Education agreed to make a grant of £126 and a new floor of Tasmanian oak was laid at a cost of £380. Hitherto the seating had been provided by a number of wooden chairs from the old wooden hut and a few cinema seats. In 1950 the hall committee purchased 150 stacking chairs.

Later, when the village school was enlarged and kitchens built, the need of the hall by the County Council was over and the hall was vacated with an ex gratia payment of £50 for dilapidations.

The hall funds continued healthy and the hall has been kept in a good state of repair and decoration by the village hall committee. It is now recognised as one of the better village halls in the county. More chairs were donated by the Ropley Silver Jubilee Committee in 1977, and the accommodation and equipment is constantly being improved and can now meet the requirements of almost any social occasion. The stage with its facilities has been the centre of many a fine production by the Ropley Amateur Dramatic Society, and the Sequence Dance Club nowadays use the large hall every week. Other regular users are the Playgroup and Youth Club, and talks, jumble sales, Church Fayres, Harvest Suppers can all be accommodated, to say nothing of wedding receptions and discos.

Church Street Cottages today

ROPLEY FC in their first season, 1899-1900
Standing (*l to r*): Jim Hale, Tommy Turner, Bill Hall, Charlie Harding, Mr Robinson (*referee*), Phil Forde
Seated (*l to r*): Alf Hale, Jack Hall, Tommy Gaiger, Frank Budd, Alf Gaiger

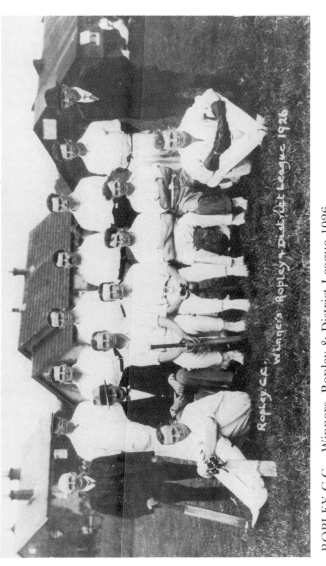

ROPLEY C.C. Winners, Ropley & District League 1926
Standing (*l to r*): RC Turner (club secretary), 'Arch' Hale, (?)Cyril Forster, Alf Privett, Reg Wilkes,
(?)Phil Forde, F Allen, Bert Smith (groundsman)
Seated (*l to r*): Dave Long, Reg Hall, Cyril Shelcott, Cecil Turner, Reg Forde, Tommy Gaiger,
'Minnow' Hobbs

The originators
of the
Ropley Pram Race
From l to r:
Les Etherington
Bob Etherington
Ted Fordred
Dick Newman

XIII

THE RECREATION GROUND

The fine Recreation Ground as we know it today owes its success mainly to the co-operation between the Parish Council and the Sports Clubs since World War II, and it may be appropriate at this point to list below the names of the Parish Council Chairmen who have held the post since 1945.

1945	Dr D. Gillies
1946-48	Mr E.E. Morling
1948-51	Cdr E. Boyd Martin
1951-60	Mr A.E. Guy
1961-63	Dr J.S. Happel
1964-66	Mr H. Grocott
1967-69	Mr L.O. Shier
1970-72	Cdr R.W.D. Bray, RN (retd)
1973-75	Dr J.S. Happel
1976-80	Mrs H.M. Wilson
1981-83	Mr J. Holliday
1984	Mrs H.M. Wilson
1985-86	Mr J. Holliday
1987	Mr J. Woolliams
1988	Mr J. Longlands
1988-89	Mr W.G. Corrigan

In the 19th century local cricket and football clubs depended on the generosity of local landowners for pitches. The cricket team used to play in the park of Ropley House until, it is said, one hot summer day a small barrel of beer was introduced and, as the owner of the land disapproved of the drinking of alcohol in any form, the cricket team received its marching orders. Cricket was also played on a field at Myrtle Farm behind the Anchor Inn.

As team games increased in popularity the need grew for a central recreation ground and early in this century the Parish Council negotiated a loan with the Ancient Order of Foresters to be paid back in a number of years, and the necessary land in Vicarage Lane was purchased. To enable the loan to be repaid a proportion of the land was let as allotments, leaving the centre of the field for cricket or football. The pitches often overlapped and some dissension ensued. No facilities existed until Lady Blackett of Ropley Grove presented a corrugated iron and matchboard pavilion before the first War which was erected at the west side of the ground. Between the wars a Tennis Club was formed and grass courts were laid out with a wire net surround and small club house. More ground became available for recreation purposes as the number of allotments decreased between the wars and the ground was kept in a reasonable state by the sports clubs themselves.

During World War II there was no responsibility on anyone for the upkeep of the ground and by 1945 it had deteriorated into a very sorry condition. Only three allotments remained; the field was overgrown, the grass tufty and prolific with docks, thistles and other weeds, with an overabundance of rabbits, and the hedges were wild and overhanging. To overcome this sorry state a public meeting was called after the war by Colonel H. Strong and Mr A.E. Guy of the Parish Council, which was held in the Village Hall and the Ropley Recreation Ground Improvement Committee was formed under the chairmanship of Col Strong, with Isabel Kennaway, Cdr Boyd Martin and C. Forster among its members. Mr Guy negotiated with the National Playing Fields Association and the Ministry of Education, which after many difficult meetings, resulted in an agreement to assist in restoring the ground. In the meantime, the committee had organised social functions, including sweepstakes that raised £700 in just over a year, and in a short time Mr Guy was able to inform the Association and the Ministry that about £1,000 had been raised locally.

At a cost of £2,500 and with much voluntary help from farmers Morgan, Hoff, Graham and Newman and the local Girl Guides, the ground was grubbed out and relaid, the hedges also were removed and replaced by wire fences with a new entrance gate erected by the Village Hall forecourt. The tennis courts were dug up and replaced by two hard courts with the wire net surrounds renewed. The members of the Tennis Club themselves moved the small clubhouse into place and renovated it. Thanks to Mr Guy's efforts the Ministry of Education contributed a grant of £1,500 to the total costs.

Unfortunately, the contractors from Salisbury gave little satisfaction from the outset of the operation. They had little skilled labour and almost no machinery. The former they obtained locally from unskilled men and borrowed some machinery from a local farmer. The cricket square was most unsatisfactory and had to be relaid. It was also very unfortunate, especially for the contractors, that the bowling green was the victim of a very fierce gale that lifted off the soil and seeds within a few days of sowing. To make matters worse the contractors became bankrupt. The Ministry was informed of the situation and the contractors were paid the outstanding amount.

The failure of the contractors left a financial and organisational problem requiring the close co-operation of the committee, the Parish Council and the sports clubs.

So far no expense had been charged to the rate and it was the intention of the committee and the Parish Council to continue that practice. An attempt was first made to run the Village Hall with the Recreation Ground as a Community Centre, but without success. After a two-year trial agreements were reached with the various sports clubs for payment of nominal rents on the understanding that each club took full responsibility for maintenance and repairs for their grounds, pavilions and water, while the Parish Council agreed to continue responsibility for insurances, tithes and taxes, fences and verges and mowing of the outfield. With another Ministry grant some machinery was purchased and a part-time groundsman was employed.

To help in raising funds for continuing upkeep fetes were organised each Whit-Monday from which the sum of about £100 was realised each year. A children's playground equipped with swings, slides and other apparatus was opened on the west side of the ground. With the exception of the derelict bowling green, the condition of the ground began to improve and the three major sports clubs agreed to accept more responsibility for the maintenance of the ground. Piped mains water was laid on for maintenance purposes and a drinking fountain installed, only to be removed after visitations by vandals.

The village postmaster, Mr L. Shier, took a hand in 1957 and led an attack on the wreckage of the bowling green with a band of enthusiastic supporters. The newly reformed Bowling Club relaid and seeded the green through their own efforts and resources, and erected a neat pavilion.

By 1960 the village had a first class cricket and football arena, tennis courts, bowling green and children's corner. The sports clubs had by now accepted full responsibility for the upkeep of their respective grounds. The services of the groundsman were dispensed with and the Parish Council hired the County Council mowers to trim the outfield.

The existing football/cricket pavilion was now too small and dilapidated and had no sanitary arrangements. It had also suffered somewhat from vandals. The Cricket and Football Clubs united their efforts to provide funds for a new pavilion and the Hampshire and Isle of Wight Playing Fields Association and the Hampshire County Council made a combined grant of £376 leaving £600 to be raised locally. Mr C. Forster presiding over a Pavilion Committee was able to raise this sum in two years and the new pavilion, complete with verandah, a large central room flanked by two dressing rooms and separate toilets, was opened on the west side in 1962. It was further extended and provided with shower facilities in 1986. Meanwhile the Tennis Club had built themselves a fine new brick pavilion in 1981 and the Bowling Club followed suit with an equally fine pavilion in 1986. Moreover, in 1984 a group of concerned parents decided that the children's playground should be improved. An organisation called ROMPS (Ropley's Organisation for Making our Playground Safer) was duly formed and a total of £8,000 was raised by way of grants and voluntary contributions. Several new pieces of equipment were installed between 1985 and 1987 and the post war equipment was renovated.

The Recreation Ground has now become one of the prides of the village. Tree planting carried out in the early 70s with the help of the County Council has greatly enhanced the appearance of the ground, and the Coronation of Queen Elizabeth II was also commemorated by a number of flowering trees. The late Dr D. Gillies, who did so much for the health of the village, is suitably commemorated in the 'Rec' by four seats bearing his name.

XIV

THE SPORTS CLUBS

(a) Ropley Cricket Club

A cricket club has been the pride of the village from the end of the last century when matches were played in the grounds of Ropley House. For a number of years prior to the 1939-45 war, Major Holroyd of Ropley Manor captained the side with popular local practitioner, Dr Oliver, as his vice-captain and wicket-keeper. At that time, the club enjoyed all-day games with Winchester City Police whilst other local fixtures included East Tisted, Tichborne Park, Cheriton, Medstead and Old Alresford. Although not an outstanding player, the village school-master, Mr R.C. Turner, was club secretary.

One of Mr Turner's pupils was Walter 'Titch' Bone who began his playing career with Ropley in 1929 and who continuously, with the exception of the war years, played for the side every year since, including the 1986 season. In 1979 the club presented 'Titch' with a silver salver to commemorate 50 years of playing and service.

Little knowledge of the prewar activities of the club has survived. However, it is known that players of note in those days were local grocers Cyril Shelcott and C. Forster, 'Titch' Bone, Fred Allen, Reg Wilks, Tommy Gaiger, Dave Long and Captain Holman. The club's big hitter was Cecil Turner, and brothers Phil and Reg Forde also contributed greatly towards the club's success. Monkwood market gardener, Percy Cobb, secured a place in the side not only for his cricketing prowess, but because his van provided transport to the away games. Bert Smith was the groundsman and it was his job to shod the horse with leather shoes that pulled the mower and roller across the square. In those days the outfield was not mown and this no doubt encouraged the renowned big hitting of the day.

Immediately after the war the Recreation Ground, which had been used for allotments, was ploughed up, the outfield reseeded and the square laid with the Cumberland turf which is the surface played on today. This major work necessitated the club playing away games only in the 1946 season. The team in the immediate post-war years consisted of several of the pre-war stars, but these were joined by the likes of Jim Russell, who always played in brown plimsolls, Don Shelcott, Charlie Forster, Graham Snell, Brian Conway, Dennis Bone, Harold Mood and his son Andrew, Bob Etherington, Frank Newman, Tom Maclachan and Privett farmer Cliff Mortimer. One of the most feared local fast bowlers in those days was 'Snowy' Bunce, but Snowy could also handle a bat very well and he scored a memorable 102 against Medstead in 1948. During this period the club was under the enthusiastic and energetic leadership of Colonel Strong who lived at 'Little Barton', Petersfield Road.

The 1950s saw a vigorous campaign to raise funds for the new pavilion, built by Kingsland & Allen of Church Street, shared with the Football Club and opening in 1962, on which occasion a concrete Don Bradman practice cricket wicket was presented by the *People* newspaper.

The 1950s also saw the emergence on the team sheets of new names such as Charles Hellewell, Richard Skinner, Dr John Happel and Dick Newman, and the appearance of a 14 year old boy, Brian Timms, for the club. His obvious talent was immediately recognised and it was not long before Ropley's loss was Hampshire's gain. Brian played many games for the county side in a long and distinguished career.

The club holds one or two unusual records and has featured in some amusing incidents. For example, in the early 1960s 'Titch' Bone travelled to an away game with Old Alresford in the boot of Cliff Mortimer's car along with the kit. Also, in about 1949, Fred Allen went out to bat with a box of Swan Vestas matches in his pocket. The unfortunate Fred was struck on the pocket by a fast ball, which ignited the said matches. In the flames and ensuing confusion, the opposition took advantage and Fred was run out.

A record which the club are proud of is the quarter century that *Snowy's Match* has been played. This is an annual social occasion where a select side, led by Snowy Bunce, turn out against Sam's Eleven, captained by Sam Rawston, whose parents used to live in the village. A unique feature of this match is that refreshments in the form of beer are brought out to the fielding side every six overs. A record of which the club are not quite so proud was established in 1949 when they were all out for 9 runs against Tichborne Park and including three extras! The best recorded bowling performance was by Snowy Bunce against

Crondall when he took 10 wickets for four runs, a feat unlikely ever to be beaten. The lowest scoring game was in the 1950s when Ropley who batted first, scored 28 runs, but managed to dismiss Medstead for 21 runs, thanks to another fine bowling performance by Snowy Bunce.

During the 1970s the team still consisted almost exclusively of village residents. Notable players in those days were Keith Stroud, Michael Aves, Mark Munday, Simon Marchant, Bob Archer, Mike Hutley, Robin Munday, Stephen Radford, Gordon Rodgers, Dave Cooper, John Happel and Giles Stogdon. Several of these players regularly turn out for the side today.

Carrying on the tradition of local builders, Keith Stroud and Bob Archer extended the pavilion in 1984 by adding on an extra changing room, ladies toilet, scorer's box and shower facilities. The cost of this work was over £7000, the money again being raised by grants and a lot of effort on the part of David Ottley.

The fixture list has not changed much over the years with the emphasis being on traditional friendly local matches held on Saturdays and Sundays. In recent years, the club has widened its activities to include competitive league and cup winter indoor cricket with the Alton Sports Centre being the venue. The Bass Alton League limited-over cricket played on mid-week evenings has also brought the club added success. Under the captaincy of Michael Robins in 1983 the mid-week knock-out cup was won. In 1926 the club won the Medstead Cup; a competition that it enters each year, but it was a long time before that success was repeated. In fact it took until 1982, again under Michael Robins' leadership.

The 1980s saw the emergence of Chris Graham as one of the club's highest and most reliable run scorers. In 1985, away at Rogate, he scored his first century—repeated several times since then. Both Giles Stogdon and David Ottley are also stalwarts who have greatly contributed to the club's successes in the 1970s and 1980s, both having been recognised by being asked to accept the post of president. Other recent club presidents over the past 20 years have been Don Shelcott, S.G. Morgan, Ian Graham, Colonel Marchant and Charles Hellewell.

(b) Ropley Football Club

Prior to its introduction to League Football, the Ropley team in its red shirts were familiarly known as the Robins and played friendly matches against other villages in the district. Village loyalty and hard living in those times produced hard playing and the matches were very often only nominally 'friendly', no quarter being given or accepted on either side. The game invariably carried on into the taproom of the nearest inn to become a convivial evening, even if occasionally it ended in a cracked head or two. The team has throughout its history contained brothers or members of certain families such as the Fordes, Hales and Etheringtons.

Following World War II the club probably had its best team ever. For a number of seasons the club played in the Alton District League which gradually deteriorated both in standards of play and quality of grounds. Several clubs resigned and joined other Leagues, but this was difficult for Ropley owing to its geographical situation. However, they applied for and obtained admittance to the Winchester and District League, enabling them to meet old friends and worthy opponents such as Alresford and Cheriton. The secretary of the Alton League thereupon lodged strong objections to the transfer which were upheld by the Hampshire Football Association. Despite the production of proof that the parish boundary at The Anchor Inn was within ten miles of the city boundary at St Swithun's School, the County Association stood by their decision. There followed a vivid correspondence in the local press in which there were, on occasions, some very harsh criticism of the Alton League. All this had no effect, however, and the Ropley Club was condemned to play in the Alton League.

The premonition of the Ropley Club was fulfilled when in the following seasons other clubs resigned and the League dwindled further. Ropley Club succeeded in heading the League, but in most seasons it occupied a position somewhere below the top position. Finally the Alton League was disbanded and in the 1972-3 season the club's first team entered the Basingstoke League.

Thanks to the hard work and efforts of men such as Bob Etherington and Fred Archer the situation greatly improved during the 1970s. In 1972/3 the team was promoted to the premier division and in 1974/5 they went further up into the senior division—the only time in Ropley's history they have played in senior football. The team stayed in the senior division for four seasons, but with the loss of some of the better players they were successively relegated and have played in division 2 since 1983.

Meanwhile a reserve side had been formed in the 1970s by Bob Archer (many of them from the 'under 10s' club), and played in division 3 for some years until it had to be dropped for lack of players. The Boys' Club was also disbanded in 1986.

Bob Etherington, who had devoted himself whole-heartedly to the club for over fifty years, died at the beginning of the 1987/88 season, and the club has since been run practically single-handed by Bob Archer, backed up by sturdy veterans, including the District Councillor, Robin Munday, and by some new young blood.

The club's pavilion on the Recreation Ground, built and shared with the Cricket Club since 1962, was extended and provided with shower facilities in 1986.

(c) Ropley Lawn Tennis Club

Ropley Tennis Club was formed in the period between the two World Wars, when two grass courts were sited on the Recreation Ground, and the club acquired a small wooden pavilion with help from Miss Ailie Henderson of Ropley Cottage, who maintained a lifelong interest in the club until she died in 1982. The courts were neglected during the 1939-45 war and were unusable. After the War the improved recreation ground was opened which included two hard tennis courts. The Tennis Club was reconstituted on 7th May 1950 and the old pavilion was moved to its present site and reconditioned by club members.

By 1957 the club membership numbered 36 adults and seven juniors, and matches were played against clubs as far afield as Petworth and Portsmouth.

In 1960 new wire netting was put round the courts, but it was not until 1970 that the much needed re-surfacing of the courts was finally achieved. It is much to the credit of the firm *Grassphalte* which carried out the work that the courts remained in good condition until 1988 when further re-surfacing took place. Since 1970 the netting has been renewed three times and in 1981 the new brick pavilion was completed, the opening date being near enough the date of the wedding of Prince

Charles and Lady Diana to justify two commemorative bricks to 'Charles' and 'Diana' being placed one on either side of the main entrance.

In 1977 a line of *cypressus leylandii* was planted by the club members to commemorate the Queen's Silver Jubilee and to provide a screen and improved background.

Formal coaching on eight consecutive Sundays during the summer has continued every year since 1970 for both adults and juniors and has proved to be very popular. Members now take part in a full programme of both friendly and league matches, with varying success. Numbers now vary around 150 members and are still increasing.

(d) Ropley Bowling Club

At the beginning of the century a private bowling green was maintained at the Chequers Inn. This green was well patronised, not only by the players but their families as well, for it supplied a much needed social centre, the beer and the company adding up to the ingredients for an enjoyable afternoon.

But for thirty years thereafter there was no provision for playing the game in Ropley, and enthusiasts had to travel to Alresford, Four Marks or Alton.

After the Second World War provision was made in the Recreation Ground Improvement Scheme for a first class bowling green with three rinks. It cost £700 to lay but the incompetence and bankruptcy of the contractors, and the terrific gales that followed its seeding, brought all this work to nought, and the green lay derelict for several years.

In 1957, Mr L.G. Shier, who had recently moved into the village, persuaded a group of enthusiasts to work on the wreckage of the old green, and as a result of their unstinting work the following year saw the realisation of their hopes and a splendid green was opened. The first president was Dr J. S. Happel and the club became a very sound one both in finance and membership under his successor, Commander E. Boyd-Martin, R.N. A small pavilion was erected at the back of the green and water laid on. In appreciation of this voluntary effort the Parish Council allowed the club the exclusive use of the green for a peppercorn rent. Three founder members of the club, Doris Longley,

Dick Cox and Jim Perkins, are now life members and actively support the club (two of them playing regularly) and Jim Perkins is the club's president (1989).

The club continued to prosper through the 79s and 80s and playing membership was restricted to 50 in 1984, 55 in 1986 and 65 in 1988, plus two extra places for inhabitants of Ropley who may wish to join the club. At the end of 1984 a plenary meeting of club members was called by the president, Sir Frederick Mason, and chairman, 'Ernie' Stride, and it was decided to launch a drive for funds to build a new pavilion. With enthusiastic support from members, and grants and loans from the Parish and District Councils, the Sports Council, Hampshire Playing Fields Association and Television South Trust, a total of over £12,000 was raised and a handsome brick-built pavilion was erected. This was formally opened by the General Secretary of the Hampshire Playing Fields Association in May 1986.

The new pavilion has provided a notable stimulus to the affairs of the club and brought in new members. Over 50 fixtures are made regularly with clubs in Hampshire, Surrey and West Sussex during the short five-month season, in addition to participation in the Three Counties League. The club's facilities were further improved during 1988 by the installation of a generator to provide electricity (the cost of which was very generously donated by a club member); the laying of a large terrace to one side of the pavilion making a very pleasant seating area for spectators, the work being carried out entirely by club members; and the installation of a modern watering system fed by an independent main pipeline laid across the recreation ground. The funds for this were raised through various grants, donations from club members, and a 24-hour sponsored bowling marathon in June 1988, undertaken by one of the club's younger members, John Goodeve, and spearheaded by the Chairman, Richard Goodeve, which raised over £1,800, thanks to the enthusiastic support given by local tradespeople, villagers, club members and their friends.

Following the improvement in facilities, it was decided to apply for affiliation to the Hampshire Bowls Association, and towards the end of 1988 the men's section was notified that their application had been successful. Plans now being considered for the future include an extension to the green to provide extra rinks, together with provision of further cloakroom facilities in the pavilion.

The club's emblem—featured on its sweaters and ties—is a beehive, reminding us all that Ropley used to be celebrated for its bees whose honey was said to have been relished by William the Conqueror.

XV

VILLAGE CUSTOMS

The customs of village life in Wessex derive mainly from a cycle of fertility festivals dating back to the Belgae in Roman times. In a letter to Abbot Mellitus in AD 601, Pope Gregory sent a message to Bishop Augustine in Britain, advising the conversion of these pagan festivals to the Christian calendar. A well known example is the translation of the Yuletide to Christmas.

PLOUGH SUNDAY: For the farmers, Epiphany was the start of the annual fertility cycle. The original Plough Monday ceremonies lapsed many years ago, but in 1948 the vicar, Peter Were, revived the festival in church on the first Sunday after Epiphany with a plough resting in the chancel.

MAYING: In earlier days May Day was celebrated by 'May Children' dressing up, wearing crowns of flowers and carrying floral garlands. They would perambulate the village stopping at each house to sing a couple of verses for which they would be rewarded with a penny. The last record of this is in 1929 when two little girls did the round.

ROGATION SUNDAY: The first appearance of grain shoots received the blessing of the church. The vicar led his choir and congregation from the church in procession to the open fields, usually by Lyeway Lane, where an open air service of 'Blessing the Crops' was held.

CLEANING: Another old custom that has lapsed. In Ropley the word was hardly known, the colloquial term being 'leasing'. After the harvest, whole families would turn out into the fields to 'glean' or 'lease'. This was to clean up the fields and very often the ringing of the church bell was the signal to begin. The leasers kept the corn they had collected, which, after being ground, was converted to home-baked bread.

HARVEST FESTIVAL: In 1843, the Rev R.S. Hasker introduced a special thanksgiving festival in his church at Morwenstow in Cornwall for the bountiful crops of the year and from this isolated parish came the colourful celebrations arranged in Ropley, as in most churches and chapels today.

HARVEST HOME: This is not to be confused with the Festival although it is celebrated in conjunction with the church festival. It has been recorded in the 16th century during which the centre of activity was an image, richly dressed and crowned with flowers. This image was made from the last bale of straw and was called a 'kern-baby', a corruption of corn baby. The Harvest Home in Ropley was revived in 1948 by local farmers at which, usually on a Friday night early in October, the villagers would congregate in the Village Hall to partake of 'vittals' and liquid refreshments. The party would usually include some form of entertainment and dancing. It has probably developed from an early form of outdoor barbecue where a beast of some kind was roasted whole over a wood fire.

'MUMMINGS' or 'MUMMERIES' originated from the Miracle Plays of the Tudor and Plantagenet periods and were usually performed in the Christmas season. The plot usually involved King George (derived from St George) Turks or 'turkey snipes', a Johnny Jack, and a 'quack' or surgeon, compered by 'Father Christmas'. Other characters were sometimes added in some districts. The plays were unscripted and handed down by word of mouth, usually in verse, but there was scope for hilarious adlibbing, and the plot varied little from village to village. The players were usually masked, and the costumes gaudy involving the generous use of streamers and ribbons, sometimes made from paper, while the principals were armed with wooden swords. Boxing Day was the traditional day for their performance when the mummers would progress from one big house or perhaps a public house to another. In some groups music was supplied on a melodian, violin or tin whistle. In

Ropley these plays were performed by the 'Christmas Boys' now defunct. The production of a morality play which took place in Ropley church, under the title of 'Everyman' in 1979 was reminiscent of those old plays

'MORRIS DANCING' became common in this country about AD 1350 and was a summer time form of merrymaking performed in the open air. It was introduced into this country as a Moorish dance from Spain; in fact the name Morris is derived from the word 'Moorish'. Two popular characters in the dance are the Hobby Horse and the Fool. The dancers usually wore a unique costume of white shirt and trousers gaudily bedecked with streamers and jingle bells. The design of the costume varied from team to team and was usually topped by straw boaters. Some clubs in this part of Hampshire have revived these dances and tour the villages, including Ropley, during the summer.

FOLK SONGS are the descendents of the lays performed in Tudor times. They are country style and very often made up as the performers sang. The lyrics were very often local in content and could also be topical. They were seldom written down but the more popular songs and tunes were handed down from generation to generation. Particular to this parish is a song entitled 'Ropley Village', more generally known as 'Greenstockings'. Miss Hagen includes a version of the song 'A Sheep Shearing' in her book *Annals of Old Ropley.*

HALLOWEEN was celebrated in the old days by young maidens sprinkling hempseed round the churchyard and singing a rhyme. This was supposed to encourage a lover to appear. In recent years other customs from elsewhere have been introduced and observed by the Guides and Brownies, in which ghosties and witches play their part and the darkened hall festooned with cobwebs, spiders, bats and owls with a parade of illuminated turnip lanterns.

EMPIRE DAY was usually celebrated on May 23rd or 24th each year, when the children marched from the school to parade before a flagstaff in front of the old pavilion on the recreation ground. The vicar would conduct a short service culminating in the ceremony of 'Saluting the Flag'. The children were then granted the rest of the day as a holiday. After the Second World War, 'Empire Day' became 'Commonwealth Day' but the semi-military parades and flag waving ended and the children lost their half-day holiday.

THE PRAM RACE is organised by a committee of local sports and other bodies every Spring Holiday Monday, and is a modern innovation founded in 1966. It is claimed to be the original pram race from which similar races have been successfully run in the county. The race was originally sponsored by Courage Ltd who presented a cup. Each pram is manned by a 'pusher' or 'nurse' and a 'baby', both usually dressed in what is remotely supposed to be in character. The race starts from the Recreation Ground where the competitors are paraded, and their prams and fancy dress judged for style and originality. They then run for their prams at the starting gun. The first stop is at the Star Inn where the competitors have to drink half a pint of shandy. Then on to the Chequers and another half pint of shandy is quaffed, to be followed by another gruelling leg to Berry Hill and Hook Lane to the Anchor and the finish. The whole course is about two and a half miles long, which includes some exhausting gradients, collisions and upsets. It is usually over in under a quarter of an hour and is followed by a tug-of-war and other events and stalls and a prize-giving in the grounds of the Anchor Inn. Proceeds from these events are usually shared by the participating bodies.

XVI

OLD ROPLEY ORGANISATIONS
(For list of today's organisations see XXV)

ROPLEY BRASS AND REED BAND: From the start of the century to 1939 there was a Ropley Brass and Reed Band with headquarters in the hut at the Anchor Inn. For many years the bandmaster was Tom Collister of Alresford, a former Army bandmaster, who conducted the band with great distinction and welded it into a first class combination. Mr George Hale, jnr (Slinger) also conducted for a number of years. During the 1930s it was fostered by the Ropley Branch of the British Legion which supplied the bandsmen with uniforms. The last band-master was Captain S. Leech of the Church Army.

The band was in great demand in the district for fêtes, flower shows and dances. During the summer it very often performed in the band-stand in the Westbrook Gardens in Alton on Sunday afternoons. It also provided the music at the Ropley Flower Show and its last performance was at the revived Ropley Show held in 1939 on the recreation ground.

ROPLEY CHORAL AND DRAMATIC SOCIETY: This Society had a powerful following from its birth, but it lapsed after World War I. After an interval of a few years the dramatic section was revived in the 1920s with the help of such 'characters' as Harry Stewart and Gordon Barnard, who is still remembered for his concert parties and dramatics (in spite of his bad stammer), his hearty piano-playing (audible across the Petersfield Road), and the sums he raised for the Missions to Seamen. They became known as the 'Ropley Players' and their plays were first performed on a rickety stage in the old wooden hall.

After the Second World War, with the advantage of a sound hall, a good auditorium and a well appointed stage, the Dramatic Society was reconstituted in 1948 by a committee including Commander Boyd-Martin, Monica Griffin (still an active member) and Isabel Kennaway, with Helene Lundy as vice president (still today).

The society went through a difficult period in the late 1960s, but since then the membership has risen to about 70 (the majority from surrounding villages) and new raised and tiered seating has much improved the conditions for spectators. At least two well produced plays are now undertaken each year, and new initiatives have included a pantomime and summer 'Revels'. The Morality Play 'Everyman' and other productions have been undertaken in Ropley Church in recent years. The society is nowadays firmly established with a wide reputation in the district.

THE ARMY CADET FORCE: Formed in 1941 by Captain Robert (Bob) Grose, this platoon had its headquarters in an old army hut on the west side of the Recreation Ground. Later the hut was moved to a field behind the Dean Farm house with access from Bighton Lane. When Captain Grose left the district in 1947 interest waned and the platoon disbanded. The headquarters became the meeting place of the revived Boy Scout Troop, until they transferred to new headquarters in the Coffee Room stables.

ROYAL BRITISH LEGION, ROPLEY AND DISTRICT BRANCH: This was one of the oldest branches of the Legion in the county, but due to a dearth of local members, it first of all amalgamated with the Bramdean and Cheriton branch which, in turn, eventually absorbed into the Alresford and District Branch.

It used to meet alternately in the Coffee Room and the Privett Bush (later the Pig and Whistle) at West Tisted. Its former president was Colonel Zambra of Basing Park, Privett, with Captain Skipwith, R.N., as chairman. The Legion in Ropley now forms part of the Alresford Branch.

ROPLEY WOMEN'S INSTITUTE: founded in October 1922 as a branch of the Hampshire County Federation of WIs, on the initiative of a group of ladies including Miss Marianne Hagen of 'Meadowside', Mrs Stuart Smith of Hall Place, the Hon Mrs D.B. Chapman of Ropley House and Mrs Phyllis Munro Spencer of the Manor House, who functioned as president for the first five years. The institute started with an impressive membership of over 150 ladies, and its regular monthly committee meetings (started with the singing of 'Jerusalem'—still nowadays sung at the AGM) continued uninterrupted throughout the 1930s and the War years and thereafter. From the outset the institute devoted itself to both outside and domestics concerns, including welfare work social activities and care for the amenities of the village. During the War much was done—with modest resources—for hospitals, savings, help for the Home Guard, Spitfire Fund, Red Cross and other needs, and for evacuee children and old people, and the institute continued as a friendly welfare and social group after the War. Attendances flagged during the 1960s and the Institute was obliged to close for three years from 1968-71 for lack of support. It was reformed in 1971 with Mrs Margaret Happel as President and became active once more, celebrating its Golden Jubilee in the Village Hall on 25th October 1974. Its monthly meetings have since continued and the Institute remains a source of friendship and disinterested work for the community, participating in a variety of local events and practical activities.

XVII

THE FARMS

A few years ago it was noted by a local resident that there were then 'a number of fairly large farms (over 200 acres) in the parish, and a good number of smaller ones with a sprinkling of smallholdings' The latter were diminishing rapidly. (A.E. Guy, 1961).

The trend towards larger farms has since continued and accelerated nationally. Owners with the ability to expand have purchased adjoining holdings and tenanted farms have been amalgamated or taken back in hand by landlords to form larger units. The main driving force has been the effective use of modern technology, which has helped Britain's farmers to become the most efficient in Europe. For economic reasons, and with Britain's entry into the Common Market, the arable sector has expanded at the expense of the livestock producers.

This has been reflected in Ropley, where a number of small units remain but most of the acreage around the village is now being farmed in units nearer 1,000 acres than the 200 acre size noted a generation ago.

The majority of the land along the A31 to the east of the village is farmed from *Manor Farm* by the Graham family, now including the land which used to be Dean Farm. The land is mainly in arable crops now and the dairy herd is no longer a feature. The farmhouse faces Court Lane on the north-east of the parish.

To the south of the Petersfield Road lies *Harcombe*, owned by the Vestey family. The land is farmed in partnership with Mr Langmead of Privett.

Adjoining Harcombe to the south-east lies *Manor Farm, West Tisted* owned and farmed by the Samuel family. The pig herd has been a strong feature of this enterprise over many years but the stud is no longer operational. Dairy cows, sheep and arable crops now cover the land.

A large arable farm to the east of the village is farmed by the Wilson family from *Lyeway Farm*. This unit has also been expanded.

As elsewhere, the trend towards the larger farms has resulted in a substantial loss of hedges and trees; but the Parish of Ropley is well wooded overall and the smaller farms with their smaller fields still help to break up the landscape.

Sunnybank Farm on the western edge of the village is the home of the Newman family and supports a beef herd, whilst the Kingslands at *Home Farm* nearby combine beef and arable enterprises.

Soames Farm, Little Grove Farm, Myrtle Farm and *Chase Farm* have all been dispersed with most of the land now attached to adjoining holdings. The last mentioned is still headquarters of the Morgan family's agricultural contracting business which serves a wide area.

In addition, the parish boasts a number of poultry units and sheep farms on a smaller scale, often owned and run by landowners with other interests as well as agriculture. Specialist nursery growers are also a feature, particularly along the Petersfield Road, where 'Lyewood' nurseries in particular have realised spectacular growth in the last 15 years.

As we approach the final decade of the twentieth century and reflect on the changes which have taken place in the preceding 90 years, it is comforting to recognise that in spite of urbanisation and commuting Ropley's main industry, farming, continues to be the main background to our village life, with its important role in the preservation of our beautiful countryside. The annual celebration of harvest festival should continue to reflect this feature of parish life into the twenty first century.

XVIII

THE DOCTORS' SURGERY

In earlier times, and certainly at the outset of the present century, medical practice in the countryside was an individual affair. The practitioner obtained his qualification, put up his plate and awaited his patients. Practices were bought and sold, and doctors often covered a very wide area and were expected to carry out a very wide range of services on their own initiative, including deliveries and even operations.

For the first forty years of this century the surgery at Ropley was housed in a small annexe at Hillside, behind the Police Houses. It was built by Dr Leonard Oliver, whose plate described him as physician and surgeon and who was Ropley's doctor until 1932. He was a big gentle man who won the medal of the Royal Humane Society for going down a septic pit to rescue two workmen on the Hunt property who had been overcome by fumes (one of whom died). He had an observatory with telescope in his garden and was a keen cricketer, whom it was wise to consult in good time before he departed on his horse for a long away match on a Saturday. Rumour had it that some of his less well endowed patients found difficulty in extracting bills from him on occasion.

Dr Oliver was succeeded in 1932 by the equally well loved Dr Dugie Gillies, a lively Scot who was disabled from a hip wound in the First World War. Two other doctors from Alresford also practised in the village in the 1930s, and the village was also long and devotedly served by District Nurse Johnson, who acted as midwife to more than one generation between the 1930s and 1970s. Her services were initially funded through local initiative until the National Health Service took over in 1948.

Dr Gillies soon became actively involved in a variety of village events, some of which took place regularly in the grounds of his home. For several years he was chairman of the Parish Council, the Parish Hall Committee and the Horticultural Society. He was also a keen and vocal supporter of the Football Club. In 1938 he bought Ropley Lodge on the Winchester Road and moved the surgery there, together with a small farm of Belted Galloway cattle on his 20 acres of pastureland.

The 1939-45 War brought many evacuees to the village as well as service personnel, involving an all-round increase in the work of the surgery and the doctor's own service in the Home Guard. By 1948, when the National Health Service was introduced, Dr Gillies had steadily built up the practice which he had inherited (with only 400 patients) in 1932, and the large increase in workload brought with it a welcome young assistant in the person of another Scot, Dr John Happel, who succeeded to the practice on the sudden death of Dr Gillies in 1952. For a few years the surgery had to be moved to Little Barton on the Petersfield Road, until the present one was built in 1955 (and extended in 1962, 1977 and 1989).

Dr Happel soon became a notable figure in succession to Dr Gillies. He became captain of the football club, president of the bowling club and a member of the cricket team.

The practice continued its rapid growth, and with the addition as partners of Dr Stephen Crosse (1979), Dr Sue Happel (1983) and Dr Andrew Isbister (1987—another good cricketer), it appeared to be at full strength, including the welcome addition of a lady doctor.

Some indication of the expansion of the practice is provided by the figures of surgery attendances (between six and ten daily in 1947; up to 130 daily in 1988) and the cost of medicines for the dispensary, which increased about one hundred times over the same period. The practice now covers about 30 parishes, and all four partners have extra medical commitments outside the practice. Dr John Happel served for several years on committees of the British Medical Association and British Medical Council, and he was made an OBE in 1984. He continues (1989) as secretary of the Hampshire Local Medical Committee, advising other doctors on a variety of problems, and an elected officer of the Society of Family Practitioners.

Ropley is exceptionally well served nowadays with medical care.

XIX

THE SHOPS AND INNS

(a) The Shops

Harding's Store pre 1914

HARDING'S STORES: This shop was situated in the last century at the junction of Court Lane and Gilbert Street. It was originally known as Heath's Stores when the shop and bakery actually faced The Old Farm House. The mail proceeded no further than the store where letters were left to be called for by the residents living further on. When Mr Heath retired in 1884 the business was taken over by Mr Henry Harding, who died in the following year, leaving his wife to carry on the business with the help of a manager. In due course Mrs Harding's three sons, Charlie, Herbert and Harry, inherited the store, which included a bakery producing daily supplies of fresh baked bread.

In those days the groceries and other goods were stocked in large quantities such as sugar in 2cwt bags, flour in 2½cwt sacks, and dried fruits in 56lb boxes, and everything was weighed up or cut separately for each customer. When a customer paid an account a pint of beer was offered to a man, a glass of port to a lady and a pack of sweets to a child. At Christmas each customer received a pound of currants and raisins and a colourful calendar. Almost every family in the village kept two pigs. The feed was regularly delivered and when a pig became prime, it was brought to the grocer who killed it and prepared the carcase. The account was settled on the proceeds and another pig put in the sty. On Sundays the neighbours brought their Sunday dinners and cakes to be cooked.

Before World War I an extension to the shop was built up to the corner of Court Lane, and the old shop was used to enlarge the storage space. The bakery was retained with two big ovens and 'bunts' of copse wood stacked in the yard, similar to a farmyard corn rick. Two horses and vans were kept and the bakers delivered their own bread during the day. In 1920 there was a red letter day when their first Ford van came into service.

The Harding brothers retired in 1946 and the shop was carried on by Mr C. Forster, a leading village cricketer, who was shortly afterwards obliged to close the bakery, and finally to close the store itself in 1963.

THE DENE STORES: The Dene Stores and bakery were built, together with neighbouring houses, by Mr Darvill in about 1909 and opened by Mr R.C. Turner who was headmaster of Ropley School at the time. It has since passed through many hands, including the International Stores who operated an adjacent bulk storage and distribution depot during the last War. The Dean Sub-Post Office is included in the premises, the postbox bearing the insignia ER VII. The stores play a lively part in the activities of the village, in the charge of John Wyatt whose assistant, Carol White, won an award from the Post Office in 1987 for successfully repelling an attack by two would-be robbers.

PONDSIDE STORES: Village stores often settle around a village pond. At the beginning of the century a small sweet shop was run by Mr and Mrs Spratt in a thatched cottage near the village pond and the Archbishop's Cottage. Mr Spratt was also postman and cycle repairer. They

were succeeded by Mr and Mrs Mole who built a wooden and corrugated iron shanty on piles on the grass bank opposite the pond, with
a flight of stone steps leading to the shop door. This was a small
provision store selling almost anything from sweets and groceries to
newspapers, sewing threads and stationery. There was no delivery service and stock was stored in an open space on the upper floor and
passed down as required in baskets or on ropes.

This business was eventually taken over by Mr and Mrs A. Wardle
who demolished the old wooden shack and erected a new building in
1968, at a time when new building in the Conservation Area was
inadequately controlled. The Wardle family ran the business successfully
and sold it in a very healthy condition for their successors, Mr and Mrs
Howell, to carry on from 1973 to 1977, during which time further
improvements were carried out. Further changes of occupancy took
place until June 1984 when Mr and Mrs W. Corrigan modernised the
store still further. Mr Corrigan plays an active part in the village and
became chairman of the Parish Council in 1988.

Mr and Mrs Mole's old Pondside Store

SHELCOTT'S STORES: This shop, which stood on an island between
Petersfield Road and South Street at the foot of Hammond's Lane, was
started at the beginning of the century by Mr and Mrs Arthur Hale.

The shop was a wooden extension to the flint and brick dwellinghouse. It was taken over in the 1930s by Mr Donald Shelcott (from his parents) who ran the business with his wife. Mr Shelcott built up a delivery service using a double purpose vehicle. He also was a keen cricketer and was a formidable partner with Mr Forster at the wicket in the village games. When he retired he closed the shop entirely and blanked in the old shop windows.

THE OLD POST HOUSE: The bow front of this house opposite the church formerly displayed a variety of groceries and general goods. As its name implies the house also, for a considerable time, contained the village post office. The grocery store was owned in the early years of this century by a Mr Morris whose business was taken over by Mr William Parmiter who also carried on a catering business. The shop was then operated by Mr Nunn and after that by Mr A.E. Chick, Secretary of the Parish Hall and well known for his 'Nardy' cakes, who eventually sold it in 1936 to begin a hire car business on the Dene. The house has been a private residence for the past two generations.

A small but flourishing saddlery was run by Mr A. Rampton between the Wars, located in Church Street opposite the village school; and a butcher's shop in Church Street, on the site now occupied by 'Mount Pleasant', was destroyed by fire in 1912.

(b) The Inns

The reign of Queen Victoria benefited the country villages in at least one aspect of community life. Many villages in Hampshire boast of a Victoria or Jubilee Hall, the genesis of the village hall, now common to almost all villages. Before this period the only centre for social inter-course in the country was the village inn or ale house, which catered for the whole family. These inns, too, were a boon to the traveller and his horse, for every 'house' had a water trough placed on the forecourt, which not only quenched the thirst of a weary animal, but on occasion also quenched the fires of an obstreperous inebriate.

THE ANCHOR INN: This large public house is just within the parish boundary at the junction of the A31 and the Petersfield Road. It once had a coach-house and stables with a water trough, but they were demolished to make way for the large car park. Though not a regular coaching station, the one from Southampton occasionally stopped here, and the publican kept a carriage and horses for public hire. The corrugated iron bungalow in the grounds was for many years the home of the Ropley Brass and Reed Band, where sometimes they held a 'sixpenny hop' before the old wooden hall was erected in Vicarage Lane. This hut was also the Lodge Room of the Anchor Lodge of the Royal Antedeluvian Order of Buffaloes, long since dissolved.

For over a quarter of a century until the late War the landlord was one George Atterton, a sturdy character, who could be said to have known all the landed gentry of the district. The Hampshire Hunt still meet here once in every season, and the Inn is the regular scene for the finale of Ropley's annual Pram Race on Spring Holiday Monday. Courage have been the principal landlord during this century, having acquired the pub in 1906 from Edwards Brewery Ltd.

The Star Inn about 1900

THE STAR INN: Situated in Hammonds Lane, in the centre of the village, this was originally an ale house, dependent like other houses in the village on water from an outside well until running water was installed after the last War. Its first owners this century were the Lion Brewery of Winchester which was taken over by Strong's of Romsey, joined later by Whitbreads. Landlords through the First and Second World Wars were Messrs Hamilton Shelcott and J. Hale, which Mrs 'Bobby' Snell (Bubbles) took over in 1948 for over twenty five years until 1974 when the present owners, John and Steffy Woolliams acquired it as a 'Free House' and made extensive alterations. For many years it has been a favourite haunt of members of the Cricket and Bowling Clubs.

THE CHEQUERS INN: Exactly one kilometre to the east of the Anchor is the Chequers Inn, formerly a regular stop for the local mail cart between Alton and Winchester. Its early amenities included a bowling green and a billiard room. Sometimes marionettes shows were performed and cheapjacks would hold an annual sale of household goods. A hilarious social event in former times was the annual competition to find the customer who could down a certain bedroom utensil full of beer.

At the beginning of the century a well known landlady was Mrs Fudge, whose slowness in delivering orders from the cellar often caused irate customers to depart for other houses where the service was a little more brisk.

Before the Second World War, the inn was modernised and the landlord, Mr S. Lesley was probably the longest serving host until he retired after some thirty years to join his son in New Zealand. His successor, Mr S. Morgan, supervised some reconstruction and renovations. Further alterations have been made by landlords since the last War, and the present Landlord (1989) 'Sandy' Sadler, has converted the old coach houses into a restaurant. The owners are the Phoenix Brewery.

THE 'SHANT' or 'WATERCRESS INN': This quaint public house in the Soke is relatively new. The name 'Shant' is of Irish origin and is derived from the Irish 'sean', meaning old, and 'tig', a house. A dictionary describes it as a hut or mean dwelling; a temporary building. And a temporary building is what it was originally intended to be.

During the construction of the Mid-Hampshire Railway in 1862-1865, gangs of Irish navigators were employed to dig the cuttings and build the banks for the laying of the lines. The gangs working near the Soke of Ropley were obliged to walk a mile to the Windmill Inn for their liquid refreshment and return the same way. This, of course, was causing a lot of lost time, and the brewers in Alton erected the temporary beer-house to supply the need. The name was the natural result of Irish use, and with the completion of the line the Shant was firmly established under that name and sign, and developed as a public house in its own right. Its name was more recently changed to the 'Watercress Inn'.

There used to be an ale house also at the top of Church Street, opposite the pond, under the sign of 'The Five Bells', run by a Mrs Privett at the end of the last century. It was known as 'Hell Corner'.

XX

SOME OF ROPLEY'S HISTORIC HOUSES

ROPLEY HOUSE on Berry Hill was restored and enlarged in the Queen Anne style on the foundation of a former house in the early 18th century. It is among the largest and most imposing houses in the parish, standing in extensive grounds across which the Pilgrims' Way was said to pass from Hook Lane to Brislands Lane. The old kitchen garden is original and is the oldest part of the property having existed for many centuries. Sadly the even older and famous herb garden was destroyed some years ago to make room for a swimming pool. A sundial in the garden dated 1652 has also sadly disappeared in recent years, though its pedestal still remains. A cellar and underground passage served the smugglers in the 18th and 19th centuries. Among its owners were Dr John Duthy, senior (died 1784), a former Clerk of the Peace to Winchester Court, a Deputy Clerk to the Bishopric of Winchester and Treasurer to the Winchester-Bagshot turnpike road up to 1773. He was Receiver General of Land Taxes in Hampshire until

Ropley House today

1784. He was succeeded by his son, John Duthy, a solicitor, probably the author of *Sketches of Hampshire* (1839), who seems to have cooperated with the smugglers in his time. The house was next left in trust to the Rev William Duthy, Curate of Cheriton, and towards the end of the century it was occupied by Mr Jacob Hagen, a wealthy merchant who owned most of the Ropley Estate, and whose daughter, Marianne Hagen, was a notable benefactress to the village (see XXIII).

ROPLEY MANOR, almost opposite the stately Ropley House. This is an elegant building in a wooded setting surrounded by open paddocks. It was originally known as Ropley Cottage until its restoration by Major C. Holroyd in about 1908. A path crossed the old property from the Old Vicarage to the Petersfield Road, and the present Ropley Cottage in Vicarage Lane was built as a dower house for Mrs Montague, the mother of Mrs Holroyd. This path, widened into the present Maddocks Lane, separated the two properties. Major Holroyd was succeeded by Mr Munro Spencer, whose wife was co-founder of Ropley's Women's Institute in 1922. Sir Alan Horne, who was an active benefactor to the village, also lived here in the 1930s. (He was killed in the blackout in London during the last War).

MANOR FARM HOUSE off Brislands Lane is a fine typical 17th century farmhouse, standing by the alleged Pilgrims' Way on the site of an earlier building. A date 1697 may be seen inscribed over a fireplace. The building is a large three-storey structure of brick filled in with knapped flints. (NB The description 'Manor', as used for the two houses above—and two others in Ropley—does not imply manorial rights, which have always belonged to the Bishop of Winchester).

THE OLD PARSONAGE AND TITHE BARN, or Decimal Grange (its old name) in Church Street. The earliest date on the deeds is 1798 but the house existed as early as the 16th century. It was about the end of the 18th century that the house was restored to something like its present style and evidently was the official residence of the vicars, though there is no real evidence of this. The last clerical occupant was probably Rev William Howley, senior, who moved into the new vicarage in the Glebe Land in Vicarage Lane. The Tithe Barn is one of the few remaining thatched barns in the county, and has recently been modernised as a residence. It was here that the grain was collected and stored for the tithes of Merton Priory (see III) or the church.

THE OLD VICARAGE in Vicarage Lane was built in the late 18th century for the Rev William Howley and his successors, and was restored and enlarged in the 19th century. In his notebook the Rev T. Woodhouse observes 'in the days of the Howleys this was smaller and more homely than it is now (ie c1880). It had a stack of chimneys in the middle. The entrance projected from the front and was approached from the road by a little straight path and a wicket gate. A lane ran across between Mr Duthy's house (ie Ropley House) and the vicarage garden and continued past the "Cottage" into Petersfield Road. The Vicarage Lane did not exist'. An extra wing, coach house and stables were added by the Rev F.H. Baring in 1891. The coach house was converted to a garage for the Rev Peter Were in 1936 and into a private dwelling when the new vicarage was built in Lyeway Lane in 1957. The house is now divided into two, named Rookwood and Monksmead.

THE FORGE in Church Street. A focal point in most villages in the last century was either the village pump or well, or the smithy The latter was always a great favourite with children who congregated around the open door thrilled at the sight of showering sparks and red metal. Ropley had such a forge until about 35 years ago. It was housed in an annexe to the Old Church Farmhouse in Church Street. Its double doors opened onto a triangular space facing the main gates of the school. The forge backed on to the farmhouse wall, the anvil handily in front of it. The work benches were under the glass panelled south wall and the tyre plate was just inside the double door. The last occupant, Archibald Hale, was a typical blacksmith and his smithy was a legacy handed down over many generations. Besides the smithy he carried on business as a wheelwright, repairer of wagons, trailers and bicycles, and as a general handyman for the local farmers and gentry. He also ran an farm in the heart of the village, helped by all his family. The Hale family is one of the oldest in the village, and 'Arch' was a jovial shrewd man, physically strong and a humorous raconteur. He ran a small dairy from the house, with his sister 'Evie' delivering milk in the village from cans hanging from her bicycle. He was also a special constable who looked imposing as he controlled the traffic to the various Ropley Shows on August Bank Holidays. Now he and his forge are gone, and only the anvil and tools remain as cold witness to those earlier days. His farm house was modernised in the 1950s.

'The Forge' (Emmet's House) between the Wars

Some of Ropley's older residents remember another Old Forge which existed on the site of the Old Manor House near Hall Place on the Petersfield Road, where horses were shod by Mr Runyard in the 1920s and earlier.

HALL PLACE, a fine 18th century house on the Petersfield Road, was originally a farmhouse with extensive lands in the area. After the middle of the 19th century farming gave way to a more 'gentrified' existence, and the house was occupied for many years by the Stuart-Smith family. It was the scene of a magnificent wedding in 1928 when the Stuart-Smith daughter, Diana, married George Evans, the prestigious Master of the Hunt, to the accompaniment of a full-scale meet on the lawns.

ROPLEY GROVE on the Petersfield Road, formerly known as 'Ryecroft', another very fine 18th century house in beautiful grounds (often opened to the public) was also a farmhouse until the mid-19th century. It was renowned as a 'smugglers store', and one of its recent owners, Admiral W. Henderson, discovered a deep chamber under his dining room when making an extension in 1928. Investigation revealed this to have been the hiding place of one of his predecessors, 'Squire' Major Lavender, a JP, churchwarden and member of the Hunt, who seems to have combined his official duties with more than a little contraband (see IX). Admiral Henderson also owned Cowgrove Farm near Ryecroft, with one of the first tuberculin-tested herds of cattle in the county. Ryecroft itself was used by the Royal Navy (H.M.S. Vernon) during the last war.

SOAMES PLACE in Soames Lane is a fine old house dating from the 15th century with massive timber framing, a thatched roof and a medieval hall with late Tudor fireplaces. It was originally known as Soanes Place and was part of the Titchbourne Estate of West Tisted.

ROPLEY LODGE on the A31 near Ropley Dean dates from the late 18th century. It originally stood well back from the road (which in those days ran further to the south) and was the home of 'Squire' Mulcock who farmed there in the mid-19th century (see XXIII).

XXI

ROPLEY HORTICULTURAL SOCIETY AND SHOWS

The Society was founded in 1895 as the Ropley and West Tisted Cottage Garden and Allotment Society, and its first flower show was held at Ropley Grove in Petersfield Road (then known as Ryecroft) on August Bank Holiday of that year. In succeeding years the quality and variety of the exhibits improved, and its popularity encouraged the introduction of various forms of entertainment including pony racing in the early years of the century. The shows continued until 1929 with the exception of the war years 1914-18. By 1930 interest had flagged, and with no volunteer to act as secretary, the shows were suspended.

In 1938 the new Village Hall was opened and fund-raising was needed to pay off the building loan. Mr A.E. Guy of Oak Cottage, South Street, suggested reviving the Flower Show with the twin purpose of raising money and reviving interest in horticulture, and the resulting August Bank Holiday Summer Show was highly successful and well supported. The Annual Show and Fete continued throughout the Second World War thanks to committee ladies working in conjunction with the Home Guard. Over £500 was raised for the funds of the British Red Cross Society and donations were also made to funds of other national and local institutions.

By the end of the war, the debt on the Village Hall had been paid, but there was general agreement to continue the successful shows. In 1946 a public meeting reconstituted the society under the title of Ropley Horticultural Society with affiliation to the Royal Horticultural Society and the National Sweet Pea Society. Its aim was to restore the Ropley Show to its former high standard. In its first year the society enrolled 150 members, and annual shows were held every August Bank Holiday, with Mr Guy as secretary, in the grounds of Ropley House, Ryecroft (now known as Ropley Grove) and Ropley Lodge. The show staged at the Grove in 1948 will always be remembered by the villagers who attended and helped there on 2nd August. At nearby Bishop's Sutton 1.83 inches of rain were recorded in 24 hours. The show was drenched with the terrific downpour and tractors were employed to tow cars away from the ringside, while many members utilised their cars to form a shuttle service for bedraggled visitors. There was little consolation in the knowledge that the Alton Show had suffered a similar disaster.

Under the guidance of the able secretary, the annual shows continued and gained the reputation of being among the biggest and best in the south, rivalling the neighbouring shows in Alton. Most years now saw the venue in the grounds adjacent to Ropley Lodge, courtesy of Mr F. Newman. New entertainments were devised: pony racing gave way to a Pony Show and Gymkhana which eventually included the Junior Foxhunter Competition under B.S.J.A. Rules; a Dog Show proved a popular section, due to the efforts of Mrs M.J. Izzard; and special area displays were introduced including military bands and army displays supported by displays given by the Scouts and Guides.

In 1959 a Junior Section was formed and in 1961 the society membership had grown to 300 and about 40 juniors. Autumn and winter lectures and demonstrations were held in the Village Hall.

Unfortunately by the early 1960s interest by volunteers again began to flag, and it was mainly due to the personality and drive of Mr Guy that the show survived. By this time, however, he was in poor health, and after 33 years of service he was obliged to resign and was succeeded by Mr J.N. Miles.

In 1962 the show, this time reverting to its former venue at Ropley Grove, suffered a bad setback mainly due to exceptionally poor weather on that Bank Holiday. This was not as bad as the 1948 fiasco but it was sufficient to justify insurance compensation. This was offset in the following year, but in spite of a special appeal in the village, volunteers began once more to fall away, and the show was discontinued in 1964.

In 1983 a small horticultural show was again held in connection with the Ropley 1983 Village Fayre. Encouraged by this event a small group of enthusiasts reformed the Horticultural Society under the chairmanship of Mr B. Ganfield. In addition to the Summer Show in the Village Hall, a Spring Show and Rose and Sweet Pea Show were added to the annual programme. Visits to the gardens at Wisley, Kew and Exbury and the Spalding bulbfields in Lincolnshire became part of the society's activities and a horticultural quiz team earned successes in the Hampshire Federation Quiz. The society is now once again among the most successful in the village.

XXII

THE HAMPSHIRE HUNT

The first record of a gentleman having hounds in the Hampshire Hunt country approximately as it now is, was a Mr Evelyn who hunted the country about 1745, the year of 'Bonnie Prince Charlie's' landing in Scotland. Mr Evelyn kennelled hounds at Harmsworth. In 1749, Mr Thomas Ridge of Manor House, Kilmeston hunted the country between Farnham and Romsey for the next 46 years. He died at Kilmeston in 1798 having raised 21 children.

Mr Ridge's hounds became known as the Kilmeston Hunt and his meets were advertised in the *Hampshire Chronicle,* listed as White Hart Winchester, The Swan Inn Alresford, at Mr Vernons, and the Wheatsheaf Popham Lane, where the Hunt Club possessed a fine cellar of port. The hunt uniform was a blue coat with white waistcoat and yellow buttons. At this time, Hampshire must have been a foxhunter's paradise with a high reputation among hunting men. The blue coated Squires when they met at covert side at daybreak found stouter and stronger foxes than today. The old downs had not been broken up and the chase in those days was over one huge sheep walk with gorse patches and maiden turf where hounds could race without the hindrance of the plough as found today.

In 1788 the Prince of Wales, afterwards George IV, lived at Kempshott Park near Basingstoke, where he maintained a pack of staghounds which afterwards hunted foxes. This was during the time of the French Revolution and the locality was filled with émigrés to whom was extended bountiful hospitality by the gentlemen of Hampshire. But it must be said that the foreigners' grotesque appearance in the field astonished the Hampshire men, equipped as they were with long circular horns over their shoulders in the French style. The meets at this time often numbered 500 horsemen, including numerous ladies who joined in the hunt.

The prince at this time enjoyed his honeymoon at Kempshott with the future Queen Caroline in April 1795 and in the following October moved to The Grange at Northington. It is from this time that the

Hampshire Hunt have always shown the prince's feathers on their buttons as an emblem of royal patronage.

In 1795, Mr Ridge resigned his mastership and the old original Hunt Club was broken up, only to be reformed following a meeting of enthusiasts. The uniform was to be the same as before. It was to be called the Hampshire Hunt, was to consist of 25 members and Mr Powlett-Powlett of Little Somborne to be the first president. Hounds to be kept at Bishop's Sutton.

In 1799, it was agreed to wear scarlet in the field. Mr Powlett however continued to wear during his mastership until 1805 a long grey coat with a blue spencer over it and leather breeches. His hats were flat with very much turned up brims to let the rain run off and specially made for him by Camis of Alresford.

On Mr Powlett's retirement a committee consisting of Admiral Calmady, Mr Kingcote and Mr John Freeman-Villebois took the management. The latter soon became the sole master and continued to hunt the country in such a style that his name will be for ever one of the most conspicuous in the annals of the hunt.

In 1817 a H.H. Bachelor's Ball was given at the Swan in Alresford, notably as marking the introduction of waltzing into the dance programme.

On the death at Harmsworth in 1837 of Mr Villebois, Major Barratt of Cheriton assumed the mastership, Kennels were removed to that place and at the same time the extent of the country was reduced to much the same boundaries as we have today. Several short masterships followed and in 1846 a successful hunt ball took place at St John's Rooms, Winchester, with 500 present. Next morning there was a meet at Cranbury with a recorded run of 55 minutes.

This season, 1846, marked the occasion of Lord Gifford taking the country and the kennels were removed from Cheriton to Ropley, where Mr Wilkinson of Alresford gave the hunt a 500 year lease of his freehold land at a peppercorn rent for so long as hounds were kennelled there; where they still are today.

The great mastership of this period was that of Mr Edward Deacon who held office from 1862 to 1884. He was greatly respected and held the support of the countryside. In 1884 he suffered a disastrous fire which destroyed his stables, and in tendering his resignation, his services to the hunt were recognised by the presentation of plate from his supporters. His funeral took place shortly afterwards at Ropley Church. The hunt servants attended in their livery, and as they were lowering the coffin into the grave the hounds at the kennels, which are some distance away, burst into 'full cry'. It was a still day in December and they were heard by all.

Another long period of mastership was held by Mr Frederick Coryton who accepted the post jointly with Mr Francis Jervoise in 1889. He remained in office until 1909. Mr Coryton formed the H.H. Shire Horse Society in 1890 with the object of improving the breed of farm horses. Its annual show was held regularly at the kennels in Ropley, and during the period of its existence 6000 mares were successfully covered.

Coming to our own times, Mr George Evans is remembered as a popular and colourful M.F.H. He started his career in the Cambridge country and proved a successful breeder of hounds. In the First World War Mr Evans served with H.M. Forces after serving as Master since 1909. He returned to resume as joint master with Captain J.B. Scott in 1926, and continued as joint master with various partners, including his wife, until 1939. He sadly died after a car accident in 1954. Mr George Evans will be remembered as a 'bit of an eccentric' and a keen shot who was always on good terms with the keepers. His kennel huntsman, Will Scott, was an expert who took an active part in improving the breed of hounds.

During the Second World War the hunt was kept active under difficult conditions by Lieut Colonel M.R.F. Courage, D.S.C., succeeded by Mr H.A. Andreae who was mainly responsible for maintaining the hunt on a firm foundation. He retired in 1952.

In 1953 Mr H.K. Goschen joined Major H. Leigh Newton in the Mastership. When the latter resigned in 1955, Mrs Goschen joined her husband with Mr Robert Jones as huntsman. Mr Goschen retired in 1963 to form his own pack of hounds at Froyle. The hunt has since been controlled by a group of members acting as masters with the policy of the hunt established by a committee, the annual general meeting having the final word. The masters in 1989 were John Gray, the senior master with some 24 years service to the hunt, Frank Momber, Sue Maxse and Lucinda Cavendish. Steve Andrews has held the post of huntsman for more than the past decade. The village of Ropley has had the unique distinction of having a pack of foxhounds for the last one hundred and forty one years.

XXIII

SOME ROPLEY PERSONALITIES

MISS MARIANNE HAGEN (1856-1932)

She is remembered in Ropley, apart from her many contributions and good works, for her book, *Annals of Old Ropley,* a collection of notes and anecdotes gained from her reminiscences and personal sources, some of which have been incorporated into this book.

For several years Miss Hagen resided at Ropley House with her wealthy parents, after whose deaths she moved to Meadowside in Church Street. A great benefactor to the parish, her gifts included the re-casting of the church bells in 1927 and two extensions to the churchyard. One of her first gifts was that of a corrugated iron and timber mission hut which was erected in the Soke during the construction of the railway, probably as a gesture to combat the influence of the ale-house, The Shant, on the Irish navvies. In response to a need at Four Marks, Miss Hagen paid for its removal to be re-erected at Lymington Bottom in 1908 when it was dedicated to the Good Shepherd.

A very strong supporter of temperance, she started the Band of Hope and the Band of Mercy. She was a worthy opponent of the local ale-houses, and to help in the mission of combating the brewers she built an extension to Meadowside and presented it to the parish in the name of the 'Coffee Room' intended primarily to be a social centre for working men and the youth of the parish. There was a strict ban on the drinking of strong liquors on the premises. (See XI).

Miss Hagen was a very keen horsewoman and when H.J. Mulcock's stables became available she purchased them and added them to the trust of the Coffee Room. Of very fixed and determined habits, she always occupied the same pew in the church and after the restoration of 1896 still sat in the same place, always entering the church, as she had done in the past, by what is now the vicar's vestry door. She used to drive around the village in a pony cart, her eagle eye searching for any sign of 'desecration' of her beloved village, such as a tree being felled (which brought tears to her eyes). She died in 1932.

MR H.J. MULCOCK (The Mulcock Charities)

One of the most remarkable characters to live in the parish of Ropley was Mr Henry Joyce Mulcock who lived at Ropley Lodge in the 19th century and was known in the village as 'Squire' Mulcock. Little is known of his early life beyond the fact that he never had any schooling and was brought up behind the plough. The lessons of thrift and frugal living learnt in his youth prevailed throughout his life. Even in his wealthier days he was seen to wear straw in his boots and his homespun clothes were rough and durable.

Despite his lack of learning he seems to have had a knack with handling finance, so that he became a farm owner in his own right. There is a possibility that he was connected with the smuggling scene, but it is known that he accumulated his vast wealth during the Crimean War, by the end of which he owned several farms and land, not only in Ropley, but Medstead and Beauworth.

He bought and lived in Ropley Lodge (now on the A31) from which he would often ride on an old grey pony or in an old world carriage behind a pair of heavy draught horses, his coachman wearing a band of gold round his hat. He had a coach house and stable built opposite the church to house his horses when he attended the services. He was unsociable and quick to take offence, and soon conflicted with the strong character of the vicar, Rev S. Maddock. Although he maintained a box pew in the church he never again used it during the incumbency of Mr Maddock.

Mr Mulcock became a Justice of the Peace and as such was always addressed as 'squire' by the villagers. He lived a lonely isolated life in the Lodge. On the bench he was very serious and administered his brand of justice with some severity. In his rough manner he was kind to the elderly and sick.

He left £130,000 at his death and his legacies included gifts to various clergymen and others in the district and £500 to the Inwood Cottage Hospital that used to stand behind the Curtis Museum in Alton. He also left sums of money in trust for distribution to the poor and elderly in Ropley and Medstead, known as the 'Mulcock' charities. In Ropley the sum of £500 was left in trust for the distribution of fuel and food on the 24th December each year.

ALBERT EDWARD GUY (1898-1967)

'Bert' Guy was a true native of the parish. Son of a huntsman and scion of an established Ropley family, he did more for the village than anyone this century, and came to be identified with practically every aspect of village life.

He was spare of frame and fiery of thatch and delivery, with a sharp face and piercing blue eyes. He had the great gift of stimulating others, and none knew better than he how to get a public meeting on his side.

He was educated at the village school, lived in South Street, joined the church choir and the Scouts, and served in the Royal Navy in both World Wars, returning to the village in the warrant rank of chief writer. It was during the last World War, while serving at Scapa Flow, that he met and married Jessie, his orcadian wife and constant support. His lifelong interest was in his home village. He became secretary to the Parish Council before the last War and played a leading role in the building of the new Parish Hall in 1938. After the War he led, with others, the campaign to extend and rehabilitate the Recreation Ground, and as chairman of the Parish Council for nine years there was no worthy cause that failed to gain his active support. Many will recall his work for the restoration of the Church, the improvements to the village roads and drainage, the inauguration of the Little Wonder Bus service, the building of the Sports Pavilion, the restoration of the Coffee Room, and the modernisation of the village school, all of which owed so much to his drive and persuasion. He served for 20 years on the Alton Rural District Council and it was during his term of office that mains water was laid throughout the parish, electricity services were improved and the first two council house schemes were carried out.

The catalogue of his activities and achievements in the village seems endless, and one can go on to quote his many years as chairman of the Village Hall Management Committee, the raising of substantial sums for the school, the church and various charities, and his active membership of the British Legion, the Discussion Group and the Conservative Association.

But he will probably be best remembered for his revival of the Ropley Horticultural Society, at which he laboured as secretary for 21 years, and for his championship of the railway. He died not knowing that his long and hard fight to prevent the closure of the British Rail Alton-Winchester line was to lead to the foundation of the Mid-Hants 'Watercress' Company in 1973.

He died in 1967 leaving behind some valuable notes, many of which have been incorporated in this book. Truly he was one of Ropley's most distinguished sons.

DAME SARAH DIGWEED (1794-1878)

At the entrance to Old Down Wood as you mount the crest of Swelling Hill you will see a thatched cottage which has recently been extended to meet for the needs of modern times. This is Old Down Cottage which in more recent times has been sensitively adapted and re-thatched. It was in the old cottage that a delightful lady and her husband lived towards the end of the last century.

In the village she was known as Dame Sarah Digweed, whom the vicar in 1873, the Rev Thomas Woodhouse, described as a 'very remarkable person, gifted with great powers of speech and clearness of understanding'. Miss Hagen, who as a young girl knew the old lady, described her as an 'upright figure, her high muslin cap as white as snow, a little plaid shawl neatly pinned across her shoulders and a faint apple bloom in her cheeks'. Dame was a term of respect from children to elderly women in Victorian times.

Sarah Digweed taught a small class of local children in her cottage, mainly in reading and writing, the latter being scratched onto small slates. Miss Hagen does not remember ever seeing arithmetic in the curriculum, so perhaps it was never taught, but the lessons always concluded with one from the New Testament.

Her husband enjoyed vague obscurity in the background, but it is known that he turned the barrel organ in church. Sarah Digweed was a regular attender at St Peter's on Sundays, always walking nearly two miles to get there. She outlived her husband still continuing her visits to the church on her own, the last visit being on 11th May 1873. The next day she fell ill and died two weeks later aged 79.

'ERNIE', The Last of the Old Time Milkmen: (1900-1957)

For 40 years, Ernie Long started his day by riding his old lady's safety bicycle from his home in Alresford to Manor Farm, Ropley, to harness Molly to the milk float and collect his churns from which he ladled the measures into his customers' own jugs. His round took him to Barnetts Wood Lane where he also delivered the newspapers which his customers would not otherwise receive, and then on to Bighton. He would be in Alresford about two o'clock and would return to Ropley at about five o'clock. He was so regular, despite adverse weather, that some people relied on him to set their clocks. For some of his customers he was the only link with the outside world and he could be relied upon to carry messages, or shoes or other articles for repair in Alresford. The children loved him and his pony and often he might be seen with a young passenger. During the winter he would return to Ropley via Bighton to save Molly from the glare of the lights from passing cars. Ernie retired in 1964 and Molly, then 29 years old, also retired to a pasture at Ropley Manor Farm. Now an electric float has taken over the round in place of Molly, but it is doubtful if there will ever be another milkman with the beloved character of Ernie.

While Ernie served the northern limits of the parish and Bighton, other parts of the village were catered for by the Kingsland family from Home Farm in Petersfield Road. Muriel served the immediate vicinity from a pail suspended from the handlebars of her bicycle which she pushed on the round and her brother, Jim, served a wider area with his pony and float. Unlike Ernie's, this vehicle was the more ornate float with its 20 gallon tapped churn from which he topped up his pail. This float was decorated and always in a very clean condition. Jim continued this round until his death in 1957.

XXIV

LIVING IN OLD ROPLEY—THE TIED COTTAGE

Part IV of this book described the Archbishop's Cottage in Ropley as having no windows in the dark bedrooms, which were reached via a crude form of ladder. There were many such cottages in the village, mostly thatched and all of them dependent on wells for their water supply in the mid-19th century and for long after. One such, for example, was 'Little Barton' on the Winchester Road opposite the Police House. It is hard to imagine how this delightful small dwelling once housed three large families in conditions approaching squalor. Some there are today who would like to return to the simple life of those days. If they could, they probably wouldn't like it.

A typical cottage in those days had its thatched roof, roses round the door and a flower garden in front. Opening the front door you stepped straight into the living room with its earth or tiled floor. There was of course no cavity under the floor and no damp course, so the cottage was cold and damp. The small window with its leaded panes filtered the light and the interior was dark. Against the side wall was a stairway to the bedroom. A kitchen range and oven were recessed into the other wall. Through the doorway at the back was a wooden walled scullery with a lean-to roof, with its copper boiler, an array of galvanised or iron vessels and a large earthenware water bowl. Below the plain window was the sink with bucket underneath.

Out in the back garden was the pump, and hanging by the door was an iron bath which was taken down on Saturday nights and filled before the fire, where the family took their turns with no false modesty. There was a sawhorse and stack of logs outside, and a vegetable garden bisected by an earthen path leading to the outside earth closet. This was a weather-boarded shed alongside the pigsty and henhouse, closed with a wooden latch, Inside was a board seat with one or perhaps two holes—for simultaneous use when necessary. In addition to the household chores there was the routine work at this end of the garden—clearing the earth closet, cleaning the sty and henhouse and feeding and watering the pigs and chickens.

The lane in front of the cottage was narrow and rutted. There were plenty of children, the boys in their peaked caps and Norfolk jackets, shorts hanging over the knees and laced-up boots, the girls in drab cotton dresses and pinafores, white cotton bonnets, black stockings and calf-length boots. These children were expected to do their stint of housework and garden chores or to go ''ooding'—searching for kindling wood. School was attended irregularly, depending on other priorities such as harvest work or on the weather, since it usually entailed a long walk across the fields. The evenings were short and gloomy in winter, lit by oil lamps and candles; and in summer the daily toil for young and old was long and hard. Entertainment was scarce or non-existent, with social gatherings in the nearest ale-house or the church, and excursions to nearby towns or villages for market days and the like were the main 'events'. The post cart served parts of the village regularly; milk was sold from carts in churns or cans; bread was baked at the local store, where flour, fruit and groceries were also to be had, sometimes delivered by cart. Church was the main social gathering of the week for most people. There were no organised games. The 'gentry' had their field sports and lived at a different level from the villagers, while the vicar and doctor did their best to serve both ends of the social spectrum. It was a hard and dull life at the lower end.

It was, as now (but much more so) an agricultural world, and one of its features, less known today, was the farm worker's tied cottage. These were a relic of a system which began with the Norman Conquest, when the reigning monarch was recognised as the sole land owner. Parcels of land were granted to and held by 'tenants' (French—holders) either for an unlimited period, ie in 'fee simple' or freehold, or for a fixed period only, ie as a leasehold or 'term of years absolute'.

The monarch granted these parcels of land for services rendered, and under conditions varying in accordance with the rank of the tenant. The senior ranks, the earls and barons, in turn granted portions of their land to their own dependents under similar terms, usually in the form of armed service. So squires holding a manor were responsible for supplying men and arms, while the men working on a manor farm, the yeomen, herdsmen and serfs, were in turn obliged to keep arms in good order according to their rank.

The Church received in its turn large grants of land from the monarch, all of it freehold, and the bishops, as Lords Ecclesiastical, were able, like the earls and barons, to grant lands to selected tenants as lease holders. Both lay and ecclesiastical manors had their farms often run by a Borsman, who granted strips of land (lynches) to their workers as well as cottages, which were available only for so long as they were in the service of the lord or squire.

Eventually the peers and other landowners were enfranchised of the monarch, retaining their lands in free or leasehold. The yeomen and serfs, however, remained subject to the conditions of the landowners, and the tied conditions under which cottages were held remained in force, as many still do today.

XXV

A WALK AROUND ROPLEY'S PRINCIPAL PLACES OF INTEREST TODAY

(See numbers on Sketch Map overleaf)

Starting with Church Street Conservation Area:
    1. St Peter's Church. Almost opposite is the Coffee Room. The present-day vicarage is about 250 yards east of the Church in Lyeway Lane.

Nearby are:
    2. The Village Pond and Pondside Stores, and
    3. 'Archbishop's Cottage'
    4. The Conservation Area includes a number of interesting old buildings, among them Town Street Farmhouse, dating from the 16th century, Laurel and Pondside Cottages, Cromwell Cottage (17th century), Sparrow Thatch (17th century), Dover Cottage (16th century), 'Fordes' (17th century), the Post House, formerly a store and Post Office (18th century), and the attractive Church Cottages.

Other notable buildings in Church Street are:
    5. The Old Parsonage and Tithe Barn, now separated into two dwellings. Believed to have been the residence of vicars of Ropley in the 17th and 18th centuries.
    6. Ropley Church of England Primary School, and
    7. The Forge, next door to the school, formerly known as Emmett's House. Dates back to the early 16th century. Church Street now continues as Vicarage Lane.

Fifty yards from The Forge are:
    8. The Village Hall and Recreation Ground.

Almost opposite the Hall, a few yards down Hammonds Lane, is
    9. The 'Star' Inn

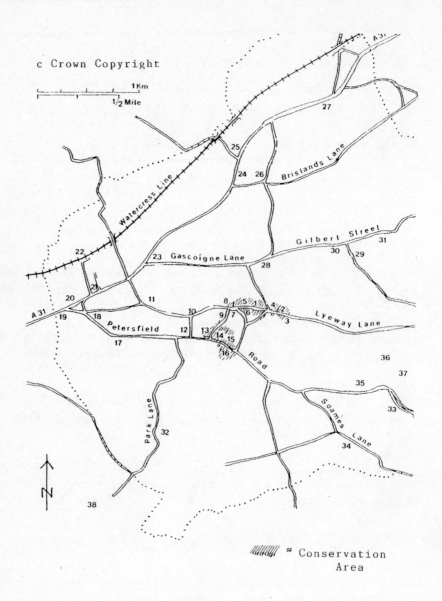

c Crown Copyright

1 Km

1/2 Mile

Watercress Line

27

25

24 26

Brislands Lane

Gilbert Street

31

22

23 Gascoigne Lane

30 29

28

20

21

11

8 5 1

4 2

Lyeway Lane

19

18

10

9 7

6

3

Petersfield

12 13

14 15

A 31

17

16

Road

36

37

Park Lane

32

35

Soames Lane

33

34

N

38

//////// = Conservation
Area

108

(Reproduced from 'Ropley Walks' 1988).

Continuing along Vicarage Lane is

10. The Old Vicarage, now two private dwellings ('Rookwood' and 'Monksmead') Built in the 18th century and occupied by the Rev William Howley, senior, father of the archbishop.

A further quarter mile towards Berry Hill is

11. Ropley House, a very fine early Queen Anne house with 20th century extension. Said to have had a long history of smuggling.

Retracing our steps, opposite 'Rookwood' is Maddocks Hill, named after a well loved and respected vicar of Ropley in the 19th century (see X). To one side is

12. Ropley Manor, a substantial 19th century house set back from the road in extensive grounds.

Turning left along Petersfield Road, we are in the

13. South Street Conservation Area. First a picturesque corner with 'Fairways', Yew Tree Cottage, Rosa Cottage and Elm Cottage.

Next comes

14. The Old Manor House, a picturesque thatched 16th century house, originally several cottages, on the main road.

Also on the main road are:

15. Hall Place on the left, a fine Georgian house built about 1790. Sometime scene of the Hampshire Hunt in the mastership of George Evans (See XXII).

And almost opposite is

16. Ropley Grove, another fine Georgian house in extensive grounds. A reputed smuggler's cellar was unearthed here during restoration in the 1920s.

Turning back along the Petersfield Road towards the A31 we come to the

17. Hampshire Hunt Kennels and Stables, and

18. 'Little Barton', a pretty 18th century thatched house (originally 3 cottages) with 19th century extension.

On the main A31 is
19. The 'Anchor' Inn with skittle alley.

Almost opposite is:
20. Ropley Lodge, a substantial 18th and early 19th century house, home of 'Squire' Mulcock in the 19th century (See XXIII).

A couple of hundred yards eastwards along the A31 are:
21. Dean Stores at Ropley Dean, with outside wall map of Ropley.

For those interested in steam railways, 400 yards northwards up Station Hill is
22. Ropley Railway Station, on the Mid-Hants ('Watercress') Steam Railway linking Alresford and Alton, with main locomotive sheds.

Another quarter-mile along the A31 on the right is
23. The 'Chequers' Inn on the corner of Gascoigne Lane and reputedly sited near the ancient Pilgrims' Way.

Further along the A31 is North Street with—on the right
24. The attractive Turnpike Cottage (formerly the Pink Cottage) dated 1745 with 20th century additions.

On the left
25. North Street Farmhouse, dated 1730 and restored in 1925.

A short way along Brislands Lane on the right we come to
26. Manor Farmhouse (17th century).

Following the road to the left we rejoin the A31 and reach the
27. 'Watercress' Inn at Ropley Soke.

Returning via the 'Chequers' Inn we proceed for a mile or so up Gascoigne Lane and Gilbert Street to several houses of interest including:

28. Bounty House, Georgian, re-fronted in 1757. Once occupied by the Gilbert family who farmed here for many years;

29. Andross Manor, a handsome farmhouse constructed from three cottages (called Sycamore Cottages) in the early 1920s;

30. Elinor House, a former Methodist chapel, built in 1869; and

31. The Malt House, originally a farm with malthouse and adjoining hopfields. The main part of this large dwelling—now divided—is dated 1746.

Finally, to the south of the parish are four important houses. They are:

32. Harcombe House, a large Jacobean style house of recent construction, off Park Lane with extensive grounds and farmlands;

33. 'Smugglers', in Smugglers Lane, Monkwood. One of the oldest houses in the village and a major centre for smuggling in former times;

34. 'Soames Place', off Soames Lane. Built between the 15th and 18th centuries with 20th century restoration; earlier belonging to the neighbouring Tichborne Estate at West Tisted and

35. Lyewood House, a fine Victorian house in brick and flint with Georgian antecedents, set back from the Petersfield Road in attractive grounds.

XXVI

ROPLEY ACTIVITIES

PRINCIPAL LOCAL ORGANISATIONS

The following shows the kaleidoscope of village organisations and activities as they appear to date. Names and addresses of those responsible are liable to change and have been omitted; they are printed periodically in the village magazine, *BIS MON ROP TIS*.

1. *Churches and Church Activities:*
   Bellringers
   Christian Fellowship
   Friends of St Peter's
   Parochial Church Council
   Women's Fellowship
   Sunday School
   Church Garden Society

2. *Societies, Charities etc:*
   Children's Society
   Cleft Lip and Palate Association
   Council for the Protection of Rural England (E Hants Committee)
   Donkey Sanctuary (local contact)
   Good Companions Club
   Friends of Ropley School
   Group Scouts
   Guide Dogs for the Blind Association
   National Women's Register
   Poetry Group
   Ropley Dramatic Society
   Ropley Horticultural Society
   Ropley Organisation for Making our Playground Safer (ROMPS)
   Ropley Pram Race Committee
   The Ropley Society
   Ropley British Legion

R.S.P.C.A.
Treasures of Hampshire Survey
Treloar Trust
Village Diary
Village Workouts
Women's Institute

3. *Local Government, Political Associations and Police:*
 Conservative Association
 East Hants District Councillor for Ropley
 Labour Party
 Liberal Association
 Police
 Ropley Parish Council

4. *Children's Activities, Groups and Schools:*
 Babysitting Circle
 Child Health Clinic
 Playgroup
 Ropley Church of England (Controlled) School
 Ropley Mother and Toddler Group

5. *Social Services and Support Groups:*
 Community Care
 Meals on Wheels
 Red Cross Medical Loan
 Coffee Room

6. *Sports and Games:*
 Bowling Club
 Cricket Club
 Football Club
 Lawn Tennis Club
 Whist Drive

7. *Youth Groups:*
 Brownies, Guides
 Cub Scouts, Ropley Youth Club